Darker Objects

Christine E. Ray
and Friends

Indie Blu(e) Publishing
Havertown, PA, USA

Praise for *Darker Objects*

"The interweaving of voices and genres makes for a rich reading experience. Ray's poems are often ekphrastic, tied to striking visual artwork. At times, another poet joins Ray in collaborating on a poem connected to an image, adding depth, complexity, and interest.

The themes are at once highly personal and universal. These works speak to us, but also for us, bolstering those involved in the creativity game: 'I see you / yes, you poet / you who lives behind the misty veil / dwelling in the border / between this world / and a hundred other / shadow worlds / ... Yes poet / I see you / ... And you are beautiful.'"
—**Nancy Dunlop**, *Hospital Poems*

"This collection speaks with a forceful cadence of urgency and dire matters, showing us the twisted underbelly of being, the arduous steps in traversing this life, and the gifts we receive from it. This work is simply riveting, all of it—showing us everything we can relate to while revealing many profound truths. Christine E. Ray's poems and those stitched together with one collaborator or many were sublime. Additionally, the combination of artwork, poetry, and prose gives the reader even more of a complete picture of the expressions in these pages."
—**Susi Bocks**, author and editor, *The Sound Of Brilliance* & *The Short Of It*.

"Ray is a brilliant fosterer of talent as shown in her contributions and dedications to several collectives and in the establishment of Indie Blu(e) Publishing. There is a tacit understanding in everything Ray does that it is as much for her as it is for the voices she wishes to amplify... *Darker Objects* is the perfect demonstration of Ray's passion for the written word and for other writers. This is a unique collaboration and celebration of Ray's ability to bring people together.

The poetry in *Darker Objects* has a vast thematic scope, and yet the editing, curation and inclusion of individual pieces by Ray, means that no voice is lost, every contributor stands firmly in their style. This is because Ray's own style, while consistently honed, is so wonderfully hers - constrained in structure but rich in imagery - and because of this every other voice is allowed to remain true to itself. At no point in the extended collaborative pieces does it seem as if structure, idea, or imagery have been forced upon the writers; instead these pieces flourish with originality and individuality, while still singing together.

Darker Objects is a sincere memento to Ray's impact upon the people she has worked with over the years. It is a reminder that Ray is a pleasure to write alongside. That Ray is a force within the writing community; a force for creativity and togetherness."
—**Kristiana Reed**, *Flowers on the Wall*

"*Darker Objects* really impressed me for its unapologetic stance on ignored subjects... I loved the poetry, some of the collaboration pieces were so well woven together they seemed like a chant. I could envision these talented writers all raging eloquently and blending into one voice. That's not easy to accomplish and it held up as a document of unity and outrage. We learn when we hear these stories, even in poetic form, and we grow from them... this is the kind of book I would recommend to my clients and gift to my friends. Pass it on, it will be so worth it."
—**Jodi Roberts**, Psychotherapist, LPC, NBCC

"Christine Ray's collection is enhanced by those writers who collaborated with her, but my favorite pieces are Ray's solo work, which act as doorways to the more intense collaborations. All build on each other, forcing the reader to examine themselves, alongside the unfettered societal neglect that demands change but isn't changed...This is a feminist treaty that will greatly add to the modern canon of women courageous enough to speak unfiltered truths... I was greatly moved by her alacrity, intensity and ability to shift me into varied emotions throughout reading. I came away full of ideas, enraged all over again at inequity and unwilling to look away. I'm glad women hold the torch for these neglects because without that we're lost. *Darker Objects* is a marvelous foray into today's world, evoked in multiple voices, disparate but ultimately united."

—**Didi Artier**, Artist, Writer, contributor to *SMITTEN This Is What Love Looks Like*

"*Darker Objects* is a culmination in part, but without ending, for the collaborative power of writers Christine Ray has worked with. In the indie market such writers are often fragmented by time and space. *Darker Objects* unifies into one different but collected voice, a myriad of thoughts on necessary subjects. When we speak out about racism, sexism, social justice, politics, we get out of the comfortable armchair and demand change. Writers achieve this singularly but when they combine their efforts, the effect is palpable. *Darker Objects* possesses this urgency and alongside some finely written pieces by Ray, the collaborations act as sign-posts and alarms, to an indifferent world."

—**Belinda Roman, PhD.**, Professor, Economist, President of SABES, Director of Mexican-American Studies, Coordinator of Texas Latino Policy Symposium

"At times it is like listening to an orchestra of language, with solos being taken that add to and enhance the symphony of the whole… Christine E. Ray and her friends have created a rare and distinctive approach to the art of writing."

—**Erik Klingenberg**, Poet, contributor to *As the World Burns: Writers and Artists Reflect on a World Gone Mad*

"*Darker Objects* by Christine E. Ray and Friends invites readers to feel the full brunt of the confusion, grief, anger, and shame that began before the COVID-19 pandemic and persists today. By addressing mass shootings, chronic illness, mental health, and existing as a woman or as a human head-on, reading becomes a form of healing. Humor also makes its way to the fore, particularly in "What say you, America?!" in which Christine E. Ray offers viable solutions to both gun and reproductive rights.

Forty-two poets bolster Christine E. Ray's powerful voice, and each poem is thoughtfully placed in its context. From poem to poem, work by individual poets often becomes a conversation. Some of the poems were written in response to one another. In other instances, multiple poets wrote individual stanzas within the same poem. In one of many superb uses of this technique, five poets ended their stanzas with the iconic quotation, "Nevertheless, She Persisted." (Senator Mitch O'Connell referring to Senator Elizabeth Warren when she would not relinquish her right to speak.) Each poet brings a different perspective to reach that concluding line. "

—**Rachel Kobin**, Greater Philadelphia Writers Workshop Studio, contributor to *As the World Burns: Writers and Artists Reflect on a World Gone Mad*

"Darker Objects is a haunting well of enchanted, gothic ink. I willingly drowned in the enchanted poems with wanton delight."
—**Trisha Leigh Shufelt**, *Ghosts of Nevermore*

"There are not enough superlatives for Christine E. Ray's newest collection of poems, *Darker Objects*... In "We Cannot look Away: Not another seventeen, Not another one" Christine and ten other poets memorialize the victims of the Parkland School massacre with: "bullet perforated backpacks/ spilling loose-leaf lined paper, textbooks onto blood stained sidewalks/ helicopters hovering to give us the birds eye view...It doesn't add up, the physics, the social studies, introduction to business, life and death 101..." Some readers might question the relevancy of including a piece about Parkland, however relevancy is unquestionable, considering the heartbreak of Uvalde and the number of mass shootings still happening daily. It is an agonizing outcry of grief and a call to action. In "The Color of Our Rights," Christine leads her chorus of talented poets, singing, "I will wear crimson for their lifeblood/ that will spill in back alleys/ that will stain wire hangers/ or knitting needles/ other unsterilized implements that become their only choice...," creating a heart-rending plea and yet, at the same time, a demand for action by the end of the work. These collaborative works are not cold, abstract experimental pieces. These are vast musical choral pieces, functioning as a powerful Greek chorus, resonating with grief and outrage, piercing us with raw emotion to spark us into action to create a better place for ourselves and our children..."
—**Annette Kalandros**, *The Gift of Mercy*

"Underlying themes are sewn together with a single word that reappears as a gentle reminder and as a way to propel the poetic narrative further. The poems find refuge in your heart and beg you to turn page after page, like a novel you cannot put down or an

enthralling symphony that keeps you in your seat awaiting the next set of sounds from the orchestra... *Darker Objects* is a collection of poems that begs rereading, as each read brings you to new places."
—**Danielle Wong**, *Bubble Fusion*

"Christine E. Ray and Friends have created a thought-provoking compendium in *Darker Objects*. Words create a bridge to deepening levels, and I became immersed, experiencing the grief, the rage, the chaos of our times. As the words stirred ever more powerful feelings, and my next breath seemed hard, the photography of Elijah R. Carney invites me to stillness. To settle. To let the imagery in and touch the soft spots in my heart and soul. And, then, I read on, to appreciate the talents of those who can distill these dark times into shining, succinct works of art."
—**Jan Abramson**, MS, (Ret), Charter Fellow, National Organization of Research Development Professionals (NORDP), mentor, community volunteer

"This is a beautiful book. The poetry and the pictures marry well. It almost has a soft gothic feel to the book, but not in a depressing way. I admit I couldn't stop reading it as soon as I got it and then I wanted to go back and read it all over again."
—**Patricia Harris**, Xactly Poetic

"The beauty of *Darker Objects* is that you can open it to any page and there you will find compelling poetry, several prose pieces, art photography, and photos of art and 3D works. Each serves to pull you in and get you hooked. Soon enough you'll be turning the page for more. And *Darker Objects* is an important and wide ranging work. Poet and artist Christine E. Ray writes with razor-edged clarity; nobody imbues prickly, pithy lines with more glee. I found myself rereading and savoring the venom she dispatches

in many verses. But unexpectedly Ms. Ray can turn around and offer poems that ache of exquisite, indelible loss. That she opens herself to reader in such vulnerable, quietly beautiful poems as "Winter's Garden" and "Peter Pan (In Memory of Dylan)" make it clear that Ms. Ray is a formidable writer...My favorite among the collaborative efforts is the take-no-prisoners collective, "Are You Fucking New Here?", where each writer gets her say. "New Here" is almost giddy in its wielding of power."
—**Victor Raines**, Writer and Art Director

For information, address
Indie Blu(e) Publishing
indieblucollective@gmail.com

Paperback ISBN: 978-1-951724-23-8
Hardback ISBN: 978-1-951724-24-5
eBook ISBN: 978-1-951724-25-2
Library of Congress Control Number: 2023947330
Indie Blu(e) Editorial Team:
Candice Louisa Daquin
Victoria Manzi
Christine E. Ray
Elijah R. Carney
Cover Design: Mitch Green

Acknowledgements

Candice Louisa Daquin- This book would simply not exist without you. Thank you for the much-needed kick in the pants, your dogged persistence, your exceptional editing, as well as your patience, flexibility, humor, healthy doses of profanity, and your deep friendship. This may not be the book you originally envisioned, but I am so grateful that you gave me the space, strength, insight, and support to let it become this beautiful, and beautifully dark, tribute to creative synergy.

Victoria Manzi- From the moment you joined Indie Blu(e) Publishing, you have felt like you have always been here, and were always meant to be here. I am delighted to watch you grow as our Promotion & Marketing Specialist and as an emerging editor. I firmly believe that there is a writer inside of you bursting to take flight, and I look forward to hearing her voice.

Elijah R. Carney- Thank you for jumping in feet first when I said we needed help at Indie Blu(e) and for letting Candice, Victoria, and I talk you into so many things you have never done before. It is an honor to collaborate with you on Darker Objects and to share your gorgeous photography with the world.

Jharna Choudhury and Georgianna Grentzenberg- I am so grateful that you agreed to collaborate with me on this project. Thank you for your patience and sense of humor as I dug through the images you sent me, as well as your social media accounts, looking for just the right pieces to make the words sing. You make this book, and the world, a more beautiful place.

Kindra M. Austin, Kim D. Bailey, Ward Clever, Susan M. Conway, crystal x, Candice Louisa Daquin, Sarah Doughty, OldePunk,

Michael Erickson, Rachel Finch, Devereaux Frazier, Stephen Fuller, Nicholas Gagnier, Iulia Halatz, Saide Harb-Ranero, Quatrina Hosain, Rachael Z. Ikins, Sun Hesper Jansen, Rana Kelly, Erin L. King, Mandy Kocsis, Aakriti Kuntal, John W. Leys, Lois Linkens, Nicole Lyons, Jamie Lynn Martin, Devika Mathur, Nathan McCool, S.K. Nicholas, Dom Wynette, Jack Neece, Allister Nelson, Jesica Nordase, Basiliké Pappa, Zelda Raville, Lynn Devora-McNabb, Kristiana Reed, Megha Sood, Eric Syrdal, Marcia J. Weber, Robert Wertzler, and Laurie Wise- Thank you for choosing to join your voices with mine over the years. I am endlessly grateful for your creativity, talent, inspiration, and friendship. I am in awe at the volume, as well as the quality, of work we have produced together. It has been a joy to watch this tribute to our collective voices take shape.

Jan Abramson, Didi Artier, Susi Bocks, Nancy Dunlop, Patricia Harris, Annette Kalandros, Erik Klingenberg, Rachel Kobin, Victor Raines, Kristiana Reed, Jodi Roberts, Belinda Roman, Trisha Leigh Shufelt, and Danielle Wong- I humbly thank you for the time you spent reading this unusual and rather lengthy manuscript and writing your thoughtful reviews. Experiencing *Darker Objects* through your eyes has been illuminating, humbling, affirming, and sometimes, even made me laugh out loud. Your advanced reviews are indeed a gift.

Kevin, Elijah, Al, and Chris- My bubble has been very, very small since lockdown started in March of 2020. I am grateful every day that you are my family and that I have been surrounded by those I really like, as well as love, during these challenging last few years.

Dedication

To all the mad-talented writers and artists who collaborated on these pieces so close to my heart and prevented me from raging and grieving alone.

Contents

Prologue

As I write this, I am struck by the irony. Any writer or editor who has ever worked with me knows that I am not a fan of Author's Notes or writer-written Introductions. I am a selfish reader of poetry and prose. I vastly prefer to experience the language for myself, with no set expectations or careful author guidance. I want to discover a piece's secrets and meaning for myself. To find its resonance and meaning to *me*. Poetry is deeply subjective. What the writer intends is important, but how it speaks to me as a reader and resonates with my own experience is where its real value lies.

My brilliant friend and editor Candice Louisa Daquin has been gently encouraging me to put out a third collection of poetry and prose for several years. The first couple of times she brought up the idea, I pretended I didn't hear her, hoping she would forget about it. Most of my creative energy has been devoted to editing, publishing, and promoting other people's work since Indie Blu(e) Publishing launched in 2018. My identity as a writer with something interesting or valuable to say felt very remote.

In the summer of 2023, Candice reminded me a little less gently that I should put out another book. I grumbled a bit more but decided to humor her and revisit my newer writing. It wasn't a *bad* body of work, but it didn't quite seem to add up to a book that excited me creatively or have the cohesion that my previous two collections did.

And then I had an idea. One of *those* ideas. What if I took this handful of standalone poems and prose and combined them somehow with some of the writing collaborations I had done over the years with other creatives? These duets, larger collaborations, and call and response pieces have always been near and dear to my heart, but they had never been published in print before.

Maybe, I thought, *there is a larger story here to tell.*

I started digging through my writing files and all the WordPress blogs I have co-curated since 2016. A lost long weekend later, I had a 240-page first draft of a manuscript entitled *Darker Objects* that wove my standalone writing with poetry and prose from 42 (!!) other mad-talented writers. Forty-two writers who had been willing to join their voice to mine in some way. *This* was a manuscript that excited me creatively. *This* was the manuscript that told a larger story.

Each of these collaborations has its own background story. Some started with a single thought-provoking stanza, such as 'Recombinant Selves' and 'Unheard Incantations' that I simply didn't know what to do with. Others are call and responses, such as 'A Response to a Poet's Love Song', a piece written by Steven Fuller after his first stumble onto my blog, *Brave and Reckless,* that has led to a deep and abiding friendship and writing partnership. Although Steve and I have dramatically different writing styles, many of the pieces we have written over the years are so seamless that we no longer can recall which of us wrote each line or stanza.

Many of the pieces in the 'American Gothic' section were inspired by themed writing prompts that I posted online to inspire other creatives. 'I Am the Woman' was such a prompt that led to many stunning standalone pieces. 'Careless Whisper' (George Michael), 'Back to Black' (Amy Winehouse), and 'A Room So Still and Silent' (Chester Bennington) are heartfelt tribute pieces to lives lost far too soon.

Kindra M. Austin's raw, fierce, and authentic 'I Knew My Worth' inspired an organic avalanche of response pieces when it first appeared on WordPress, resulting in some of the finest and most incisive writing I have ever read. Anthems such as 'We Cannot Look Away', 'With Clenched Fists, I Rage', 'Nevertheless, She Persisted',

'Testify', and 'The Color of Our Rights' were written fast and furiously in the moment, as we reflected on the world unfolding around us.

I simply do not like to rage or grieve alone.

Darker Objects felt somehow unfinished without visual art to either reflect (or refract) the powerful, unapologetic writing. All the writers involved with the book were invited to collaborate on the visual art. I also reached out to brilliant young embroidery artist Jharna Choudhury, my sister in floss, as well as mixed-media artist Georgianna Grentzenberg, a dear friend whose art pieces are scattered around my house, and photographer Elijah R. Carney. I have been avidly following Elijah's journey as a photographer since he first held a camera. Even at eleven, my oldest had a great eye.

We are unique creatives with 46 distinct styles, with 46 different life experiences. We live in 7 different countries. We are different genders, sexual orientations, races, and ethnicities. Our ages range from our 20's to our 70's. But in *Darker Objects* we are united in our passion, our rage, and our grief. We are united in our creativity and in our shared humanity.

We are unique.

We are united.

May you find meaning and resonance for yourself within these pages.

American Gothic

Frankenstein; or, the New Prometheus

stitched carefully together
from odd parts
of other women
you preferred me to be
you recklessly called forth
roaring thunder
flashes of lightning
that wracked through
my body
electric agony igniting a spark
of independent life
I rose from the table reborn
something new
something *other*
you gazed upon me,
your creation,
not with love
not with compassion
but with revulsion
with horror
you had longed for the
perfect rag doll to pose
to toy with…
we both knew
the moment
my mismatched eyes
met yours

I was not she

We Have Always Lived in the Castle

we have always lived in the castle
safely nestled behind
thick stone walls
tall metal gates
their wickedly pointed tips
razor-sharp
murky moat full of frogs
turtles & koi

we have always lived in the castle
playing tag
hide and seek
in dusty rooms
with the living
and the dead
we are never lonely
here
we bathe by candlelight
beside the cozy kitchen hearth
carefully comb the tangles
from each other's hair

we have always lived in the castle
keeping ourselves
to ourselves
rarely venturing past
the grounds
to visit the nearby village
some could call 'quaint'
deliveries received
at the property line

Mondays and Thursdays, please
we will meet you
with our wheeled wagon
we do not welcome guests
or strangers
gladly
not all of our skeletons
safely hidden in closets
or buried six feet below
the shade of willow trees
the unsuspecting are hurried
quickly back to the road
they mustn't disturb Father
or other dark things
that dwell here

we have always lived in the castle
for us—

it is simply home

Crumbling Foundations
Elijah R. Carney

Demonized

I do not speak
with forked
tongue
yet
you damn me
a demon—
paint my hands
blood red
cut me
black diamond
hard
innocent
misunderstanding?
or sleight
of hand
designed
to dazzle
distract
from tarnish
spreading
on your halo
rust growing
on your
wings?
truth
in the crystal ball
remains
veiled
cloudy
I tire
of this

unholy role
you have
assigned me
I did not
audition
for your
drama—
want no part
in this
passion play

Shifting Sands

high noon sun
baked sand
under tanned bare feet
cousins 4 and 8
bright plastic buckets in hand
aching call of the gulls
stranger at the corrugated pipe
where water flows clear
salt free
down to ocean's taboo edge
they are not allowed to go there alone
dangerous they are told
but adults congregate, distracted
yards away
by their dime store novels
cryptic conversations
that bore them to tears

silent parallel digging
in the deep sand with strange girl
few words exchanged
something about her eyes
unsettling
building ephemeral castles
before knocking them down
again
and again
tired of this ritual
her 8-year-old eyes slide toward shore line
incoming tide hypnotizing
tugging at her navel

7

so tempting to drop her shovel
walk out where it isn't allowed
stick her foot into the ice cold
Atlantic water
and just keep walking
no looking back
mermaids
calling her home

Wonky Seascape
Pieced & quilted by Christine E. Ray

The Little Stranger

we came to forget
hoping distance
time
could ease our grief
fewer reminders
around us
of what was lost
to stop us dead
in our tracks
paralyze us
with longing
but we merely
traded one house
of sorrow
for another

glimpses of you
caught from the corner
of an eye
echoes of your
footsteps down
long hallways
childish laughter
filled with delight
the lingering aroma
of rich earth
you dug your
fingers deeply into
long ago
fragrant grasses
you rolled in

pale hair warmed
sweetly by the sun
a little stranger
who never left
these walls
never moved on
haunting us
leaving us unsure
whether you
fill us with dread
or whether
secretly
we welcome you

Lost Ball
Elijah R. Carney

Spare and Found Parts

you may have
my heart
I do not
need it
anymore
I have replaced it
with clockwork elegant
diamond hard parts
it ticks faithfully
reliably
beneath my ribs
never a flutter
nor a cry
does it utter
I hold fast
to my spine
so lately reinforced
with razor wire
steel rods
I do not
intend
to ever bow or
bend
again
to the charms
the whims
of mercurial lovers

Demon Duet
with Stephen Fuller

Dancing in the dark
with the demons in my head
I lead, they follow
our steps familiar, practiced
shall we waltz, foxtrot, tango?

I should have refused
told them my dance card was full
But they know me well
I always slip willingly
into their poison embrace

The demon whispered back
Where have you been?
I waited in the usual spot
Knew it would just take time
I am patient for my dancer
She dances like no other

Tried to refuse me again?
I would laugh, but we know
my laughter only rides our rhythm
while you try to slip
poison in my sweet tea,
Again

Demon Lover

he is stealthy as the night
slipping through
bedroom windows
bare feet leaving
faint impressions
in the rug
he likes to inch
the covers down slowly
oh so slowly
from my body
as he whispers
with forked tongue
the games he wants
to play tonight
I tell him one day
I will lock my windows
hang a crucifix
on the wall
sprinkle holy water
around the room…
this just makes him laugh
as he slides confidently
into my bed

Something Wicked in the Clouds
with Stephen Fuller

Ever been cloudbusting?
We lay on our backs
in damp fragrant grass
Look up at the sky
to trace a dream that seems
soft and fluffy
like cotton candy

We point up at rabbits
and dragons in the mist
Discerning ghost ships in full sail
Moments so sweet kids swallow
them in their first sugar-filled
carnival step to torment parents
Filled with a need for one still moment
to spite the chaos. Life

Invent a new game from shadows
North winds blow in ominous clouds
We bust them up into Grimms
that twist into dark corners
Where Freud conjures out
nightmares stripping bliss
exposing naked fears
that freeze children in their place
We watch vaporous Hell Hounds
chase fleeing maidens
Giant toads swallow koi

Release our ids, wild and feral
Join the Wild Hunt
chase the devil
across the night sky
A hero or a demon
Determined by the color
of the rain that drips from
his wounds

Originally published by the *Sudden Denouement Literary Collective*

Solitary Flight
Elijah R. Carney

Winter's Garden

in deep winter's hush
branches rendered
delicate, white
finger bones
slumber under ferned frost
sway gently
against spiked leaves
thin and
crisp
as spun sugar
my December garden
sparkles softly
in slivered moonlight
as if brushed
by snow queen's
bloodless kiss

Dangerous Thoughts

My mother hovers above the 55 miles-per-hour speed limit, cigarette casually in hand. The ever-present open bag of spice drops on the dashboard melts lazily in the afternoon sun. It doesn't matter. Despite the variety of jewel tones contained in the bag, whenever I cautiously try one they all taste the same. I prefer them warm and gooey to the rock hard of overcast winter days when it would be easy to break a tooth on one.

My grandmother dozes in the passenger seat. She will deny this vehemently when we arrive at our destination, insisting that she was only 'resting' her eyes, but her soft snores give her away. We have done this drive many, many times. The exits along the Mass Pike are far apart on this stretch and there is little to look at other than the monotonous pines that line the side of the highway and the concrete dividers that keep us separated from the steady traffic heading East.

I am sprawled across the back seat, my 12-year-old head resting against the inadequately padded window frame. The sound of the station wagon's tires crunching across the road's surface is hypnotic. I am drowsy, my thoughts drifting. I idly note the mile markers as they briefly come into focus.

Out of nowhere, I am filled with the sudden, overwhelming impulse to open the car door my weight rests against and let myself fall onto the road. I envision my head splitting open like an overripe melon as I hit the asphalt or perhaps it would be the cars behind us that would do the job. Would my bones crunch or would the cars simply make a soft thud as they one by one run over my increasingly unrecognizable body? I picture the looks of horror on the drivers' faces when they realize the inevitability of the impact, but I can feel nothing but detached curiosity. I have no compassion, no guilt for the trauma I might cause nor for my family's imagined grief. Nothing feels real but the beat of my pulse in my ears.

The compulsion is so strong that my fingers curl in readiness to grab the door handle and fling it open. Fortunately- or unfortunately- the door is locked. Before I consciously decide if I truly want to unlock it, my mother notes casually from the front seat that we are less than a half-hour from my aunt's house. Pulled back from my trance, the car is suddenly warmer, the road louder, the smell of cigarettes and anise stronger than it had been a moment ago. As my grandmother's snores break off at the sound of my mother's voice, I straighten in my seat, moving slightly away from the car door, hands resting in my lap. I am both horrified and filled with euphoria at how close I had dangled at the edge.

I tell no one, equally concerned that no one else has moments like this or that *everyone* does.

Cat Nap

with Lois Linkens

sleep stalks me, finds me an easy target
slinks in to drag me under, into the depths
where unknown dangers lurk in my unconscious
what murkiness lies behind my drooping lashes,
what shadows hide between each whistling breath?
what sharpness snuggles buried
among the feathers in my pillow,
what traps will soon ensnare
and dangle me, just feet from death?

they hook me, by the ankle
and suspend me from the tree of dreams,
around which serpents rattle, tigers prowl,
insects scuttle, poisonous, foul.
blood rushing to my head
cheeks flushed
heart thundering
as i dangle helpless

great cats bat their armored paws
at my flailing hair
like beggars round a campfire.
their claws pull and snag—
draw drops of blood
that quench night blooming jasmine
waiting below

i wake with a start. temples throb and pulse,
the bed is dry as my parched throat, blankets cold.

perhaps a girl
can be herself without the hair of fairytales

Originally published by the *Sudden Denouement Literary Society*

Wonder
Georgianna Grentzenberg

Night Rolls Over
with Stephen Fuller

This still, lonely hour
removes our masks
strips us to bone and shadow
Angels dance naked
on moonlight laughing
underneath waterfalls
Cold water drips
from goose pimples
invoking hidden Gods within us
We grab hold of a wing
rip a feather from its rib
and dip it into the falls
Let icy ribbons ink our skin
carve new features
into the alabaster face
We focus moonlight
on dried skins
and let them catch fire
The flames that singe
into our naked shadow
dance like holy spirit inside
Our night rolls over
onto its backside
holding down the day

Carved

Elijah R. Carney

Ghosted

Peter Pan
In memory of Dylan

an image of you
lingers at the edges
of my vision
lurking
waiting patiently
to catch me unaware
punch me
in the solar plexus
hard
fierce
I see you straddling
no-man's land
at top of the jungle gym
late afternoon sun basking
your golden curls
into a halo
feet firmly planted
in worn, dirty sneakers
arms defiantly folded
across fragile cage
of your chest
there is some
mischief
in your challenging gaze
but there is also
something
else
that haunts me
you are not simply

testing rules
authority
but seek boundaries
limits
desperate
to feel
safe
did I pass your test
that day?
I feel gutted
ten years later
to learn
you are gone
have been
since August
news from southern
states
slow to travel
I google
with incredulous
fingertips
dig deeply
into shifting soil
of Facebook
Instagram
unearthing
incomplete
jigsaw puzzle
of your short life
and death

Composition of a Woman

grief
the connective tissue
webbed between
each bone
dangles unresolved
from bleached ribs
marbled shreds of tissue
ruffling the edges
of my open chest
cavity
simultaneously
both
obscene and
achingly lovely
rage
the iron in
the blood
that travels
twisty veins and
arteries
in an endless
roller coaster loop
sometimes gentle
but often fierce
crashing
roaring
in ears drums
that rupture
bleed
composition of
a woman

I Beseech Thee (View 1)
Elijah R. Carney

Ghost Stories

my dead
haunt me nightly
in technicolor dreams
rich with detail
texture
surround sound dialogue
seemingly unaware
that they have passed
beyond the veil
only dwelling here,
in my fertile unconscious
is it bad etiquette,
I wonder,
to point out that
they are Dearly Departed?
does Miss Manners have guidelines
for social interactions
with poltergeists
with sleepless spirits?
seems rude somehow
to bluntly point out
you're dead, you know
insensitive
discourteous
ironic
as they seem
so vividly alive
it gives me pause
makes me wonder
if the message they carry
is how easily someone

like me
can declare them dead
while simultaneously
deluding myself
that I still breath
my heart still beats
long after blood
has frozen solid
in my veins

Things that Linger

there is no need
for you
to summon
my ghosts
they always
hover near
shimmering afterimages
at my vision's periphery
murmur low
incessant
in curve
of my ears
silver inhale
and exhale
of my breath
static electricity
brushing against
nerveless fingertips
pack up
your chalk
crystal balls
Ouija boards
smoldering sage
you are not
needed
here

Alabaster

who am I
without my losses
without my ghosts
to haunt the hours?
grief has carved me
sharply
since girlhood
with rasps
and chisels
unforgiving hammers
removing softness
all excess marble
until a woman
of alabaster
hollowed
shadowed
is all that
remains

Our Undertow
with Stephen Fuller

In the sleepless nights since you left
I have become a ghost
haunting lonely shores.
My restless legs cover miles
before giving out.
I am raw, ragged.

Who will walk with me through
the darkside of this morning
where our kaleidoscoped story
hovers above the water's surface
piercing me before they blur in the brine?

I clutch one eidolon
you drowsy and tousled in my tee shirt
borrowed fabric softly falling
shaping the constancy of arousal
the obvious distaff dangers unhidden.

The rhythmic glitter of dawn on the surf
belies dangers of the relentless undertow
pulls away and pulls away and pulls away
underfoot.
Swallowed milligrams of sunlight
penetrate bare boned trees, symbolic.

The onus of my salvation.
an image given
by a phantom.

I drop to my knees and see red
stains on the mica staged to process the sun.

A drop of blood escapes my mouth
lands on the salt of the water.
I taste the essence of my pain.
I close my eyes to escape
this new life of me without you.

In sleep the surf tosses me
my dreams churn in the sand.
I reach into the mud to
pull out our story
before the ocean steals it back.

Crashing Waves

Marcia J. Weber

A Tale of Two Towers
with Eric Syrdal

Locked away in a stone tower
rest of the world
fades
becomes dim memory
time loses meaning
becomes shapeless
days
nights
spent in solitude
differentiated
only by whether
I read precious books
by sunlight
falling soft through windows
that no longer open
or dancing candlelight

by this half-light
I read the words
of Tennyson
and his Lady of Shalott
in her lonely spire
whose shadow would fall
likewise across my
bitter landscape
but I've no magic mirror
to scry upon the world below
I search my embattled memory
to remember golden fields of rye

and green waves of grasses
against sapphire summer skies
here in this place
my color palette
is reduced
to the colors the melancholic
grey and brown
alternate
across flagstone and wall
and mortar in shades of ash

There was technicolor life once
music and dancing
intimate conversation
easy laughter
food delighted palate
wine danced on tongue
almost as sweetly
as your kiss
midnight words whispered
during stolen hours spent in
your strong, sure arms
before our fall
from grace
this lonely tower
this solitude
my self-chosen penance for loving recklessly
without reserve
without moderation

I could remove myself
no chains upon my arms
nor my feet

no bar upon the door
no lock
no elusive key that jingles upon
a jailer's belt
forever taunting me
beyond the oaken boards
of the door
I have no sentence to fill
no judge has left me here
this is an oubliette
of my own making
I am the architect of this place
block by block
weathered and vine ridden
but this tower is high
and i've not the stomach for climbing
nor the strength
to smash the door
and descend the stair
by torchlight

Moonlight slants across the room
illuminates iron handle of
thick wooden door
as if beckoning me
from this empty bed
where I lie under snow-white bedding
that has become both comfort
and shroud
But what awaits me outside this door?
Are these lonely hallways
full of ghosts
a hopeless maze

leading nowhere
or would they bring me
back to you?

I Beseech Thee (View 2)

Elijah R. Carney

Careless Whisper
with Lois Linkens

I am late
to the designated place
excuses ready, half-truths at hand
you are oh-so-lovely in shell pink
your soft lips offered
I kiss your cheek instead
unable to meet your guileless eyes

the bar is dark,
dim-lit by bare bulbs in jars,
hanging by wires
from the ceiling.
the smell of warm beer
cigarettes
and cheap musk
forces in

it is loud and crowded tonight
my nerves jangle
I scan the crowd half hoping she is here
half hoping she is not
this place is a favorite
you have seen her here yourself

waiters float between tables
like human candles
black and white ghosts
in a castle of money
and make-believe.

there are big men at the tables
decorated by girls
in jewels and lace

A friend of a friend of a friend
I ran into her when you were away
innocent, just a shared drink, a laugh
not so innocent the second time
or the third…

clouds of smoke
hover,
making me drowsy.
I pinch myself hard.
skin shimmers in the fogged light,
shadowed corners come into yellow,
pink, blue

I nod subtly
in acknowledgement
to the witnesses of my past crimes
their lips sealed
engaged in their own dark dealings

above the murmur of the guests,
a song begins to play.
right on cue,
your cold hand brushes mine

I spot her across the room
she is cool as a cucumber
low-cut dress, crimson lips
her look reminds me

that not so long ago I left her bed
her hair tousled, lips bruised, lying
languid amongst silk sheets

the room wavers, long girls rise
through the mist
towards the checkerboard clearing
your touch wearies me.
something is different tonight,
you are different.
you do not hold me as you once did
a wash of face
glides like silk
by us

I am hot and cold,
sweating and chilled
heartbeat hammering

turquoise dresses,
crystals, satin, ruffles curls,
mirrored shoes

I love you, sweet girl, truly
but she is my addiction, an obsession
I hate myself
for wishing I was still in her bed

people stand, silhouetted
around us
like circus-goers

I do not realize at first
that she and her friends
mimic our trajectory to the dance floor
I try to focus on you, not them

a waiter trips, glass tinkling
as it smashes like stars on the wood.
an old man lights his cigar
from a match between the teeth
of a green girl.
the air feels cold, unfriendly

I am distracted, torn
the pounding of the blood
in my ears drowning out the beat
of the music

you move before me
yet you are not with me,
you swirl in an unknown, dream place

I struggle to maintain
my composure
her friends keep looking at us, at me
turning back to her, they whisper
their laughter cuts through the din
their knowing looks sear me

I watch your eyes—
as you catch mine
you stumble, lurch against me,
table edge hits my spine

moment of truth
you see the betrayal in my eyes
my feet fail, I fall further
cause you more pain

feet stagger
chairs clatter
lights flicker
hot tears
through the dirty light
a slither of gold snaps out of sight
guilty feet
and you do not come back

I have never seen so clearly
how flawed and faithless I am
unworthy
suddenly there is nothing left
but goodbye

Nocturnes

Interpretation of Shadows
with OldePunk

Interpretation of shadow
culmination of the pale deaths
cogito ergo, en utero
vagabond goth kids thrash around the room
time slow, I don't know
I never want to go home
right here with you
I fell down again
tripped into you
spilled my soul
we are the midnight heretics
let's smoke a bowl
and talk about kids and politics
I wonder what your shadow says
I am left stunned, paralyzed
by your movement in the dying light

Friday night blues
misfits in hybrid moments
tired dustbowl town
torn blue jeans
untucked flannel shirt
skull cap cool
riding our skateboards
nowhere fast
biding time
ringleaders
of our gang of two
no need for sidekicks

when we chase
twilight shapes together
we are everything we need

Time and space seem to conform
to your every desire
You set a fire in my heart
that still burns in the next county
I tattooed your name on
my fingers with a Sharpie
and a sewing needle
That day on the bridge
by the creek when you
said that you loved Layne Staley
I watched you gather the shadows
and banish the dark
Everything stood stark
Bas-relief of your religion
I swore I would become your disciple
Following you home barefoot and stoned

comrades-in-arms
you and me against the world
things so clear, so simple
and then. . .
you are looking at me differently
long sideways glances
words unsaid hang between us
make me uneasy
make me question
make me look at you differently
a thousand exploding possibilities
our first hungry kiss

butterfly wings starting a hurricane
on another continent
we shed clothes
my tomboy armor
you lay your trembling heart against mine
on my parents' rec room couch
our shadows fuse, dance on the wood-paneled wall

Slipping into each other
like the lyrics of a Red Hot Chili Peppers
song
From a changing perspective
I learn what I thought was wrong
My head flips an ollie
This is so much better than Molly
We are writing a whole new story
into the chapters of a small town
So far into you I can hear every sound
slam and crash in our punk rock romance
Our souls laugh as our bodies
entwine
Now I know what your shadowy signs
had to say, "Come and love me fool"
Etched into my forever
on a young and hungry Saturday

Originally published by the *Sudden Denouement Literary Collective*

Turn the night On

with Stephen Fuller

Won't you stay,
my love?

Outside snow falls steady
gusted by north wind
tapping at our window
Inside these walls
a fire burns

Softly
So softly
Spread your
raven hair
upon my pillow

Gently
So gently
We will unfold
our layers
like origami flowers

Reveal the
treasure at the core
Offer it like pearls
that dissolve
on our tongues

Won't you stay my love?
turn the night on
now

Won't you stay my love?
Turn the night on
now?
Won't you stay,
my love?

As bitter winds blow
and frost grows in ferns
across the window
Inside these walls
a fire burns

Softly
So softly
Fall into my
chocolate eyes
across the pillow

Gently
So gently
I will rub
my hands across
your silk skin.

Offer the
tenderness in your core
in small gasps
that dissolve
on our tongues.

Won't you stay my love?
Turn the night on
now?

Full Moon Mist

Georgianna Grentzenberg

Uncharted Night
with OldePunk

burning water
still marks the way
home
though that is not the path
I travel today
by uncharted night
do I go
motionless movement
a note of fluidity
diachronic changes
in synchronic nuance
the language we share
is not known here
a purpose in thought
one million yesterdays
caught twixt our toes
on the shores of time
onward it flows
upward wayward waves
at incongruent velocities
seeking a partnered, rhythmic
dichotomy

we are two hearts
two souls
two bodies
who dance together
in an expanding and
contracting rhythm

of intimacy, of knowing
at times we are a
collision of fiery sparks
under a gibbous moon
at others we are the
gentle undulations of the waves
a lighthouse, a beacon
calling each other back to safer
shores
when the tides would push
us apart
always drawn back
to the place where we dwell

the scriptures we document
reverberate in the distant air
agile calligraphy
dawning across calm seas
energetic forms churning
in the skies
a word carries on the wind
a storm gathering strength
a bastard tongue
of passion
a forgotten dialect of
unknowable proportion
we force a turning of
the tides toward
the places we belong
the soft valleys where
we may speak freely
a parlance of devotion
a patois of union

in this uncharted night
we are like the fallen angels
our open wings
enfold and shelter us
as we free fall
together to land in a bed
of soft white feathers
ancient hymns of communion
deep in our throats
our duet remakes the earth
remakes the heavens
remakes us
light, joy
spills out of us
illuminating the night
divine splendor
celestial peace

chorus of honeyed
voices and
leonine roars intertwine
invoking a new order
cant in prayer to
the open waters
an ocean of feeling
in touch
communicating one word
that protects this harbor.
burning water
still marks the way
home
though that is not the path

we travel today
by uncharted night
do we go
to speak unanimously

Originally published by the *Sudden Denouement Literary Collective*

Flower

Elijah R. Carney

Midnight Precedes
with OldePunk

Midnight precedes
the dawning of you
Shadows and peaches
lavender and spices
Rare, honeyed tongue
sings rapture
my soliloquy of you

cool moonlight
carves your shadow
against stark walls
but you are smooth whiskey
intoxicating to my parched soul
cedar and pine
warm earth against my skin

From earth it begins
Aquiline movements
fostered by need
To travel without motion
Traverse the depths
of the lilac and evergreen
pools of your eyes

sacred stolen hours
we claim as our own
we declare victory over the selfish god
time
in this indigo night

where everything that is not us
drifts away
like silver dust motes

Writ of passage into
the deep dark
where our secrets
are kept by the verdant
grasses and tall oaks
Cottonwood blooms scent
the air of our bonding

we explore our mysteries
your hands
clasping mine
ground me
connect me
to where our souls and
bodies entwine
our breath rising
and falling in unison

Born unto a full moon
Platinum and diamond
we are anointed
Holly and ash
truth enchants
incantation of love
As below, so above

earth and heaven
body and mind

as below, so above
hearts and bodies
at last in repose
held tenderly
reverently
until dawn's first blush

Blossoms

Elijah R. Carney

Stirring

with Kindra M. Austin and Marcia J. Weber

your swift flowing water
elusive, quicksilver
brushes past my shores

licking
my roughing grains
burgeoning
a flash flood

tributaries
cut into earth
new veins carry fresh lifeblood

awakening me
from long slumber
longing rippling outward
concentric circles

lapping
by turns urgent
and languid
your ebb
begets my flow

see the colors of infant life
sprouting
hungry
brilliant resilience
inherited DNA

Mosaic, Beach Stones
Georgianna Grentzenberg

Poet's Love Song

I see you
yes, you poet
you who lives
behind the misty veil
dwelling in the border
between this world
and a hundred other
shadow worlds

I *see* you

I *see* those ink-stained
fingers
that hold your pen
like a lover
that fly across the keyboard
in a torrent
before stopping, hesitating
waiting
for the flow of words to resume

I *see* the permanent rings
countless cups of coffee
have left on your writing table
the chip in your favorite mug
I see the frayed fabric
on your cuffs
of your favorite writing shirt
the fabric worn thin at your elbows

I *see* those mesmerizing eyes
that seem to simultaneously
be looking through me
straight into my soul
while studying the cosmos
and gazing inward
all at the same time
I *see* the contradictions you are
your eyes are haunting
full of knowing
full of pain
full of longing

I *see* the dark smudges
under your otherworldly eyes
reminders that poets
are night dwellers
insomniacs
who haunt the still hours
who understand the depth
the texture of darkness
who can capture the qualities
the acoustics of silence

I *see* the way
words spill out of
your sensuous mouth
like pearls, like diamonds
beautiful treasures
embedded with your tears
your sweat, your blood

yes poet
I *see* you
you who makes me fall
in love with language
over and over
whose words
stab me in the heart
punch me in the gut
jangle my nerves
bathe me in your radiance
soothe my weary soul
take me on a journey
I didn't even know
I wanted to go on

and *you* are beautiful

Originally published in *Composition of a Woman*

In Response to a *Poet's Love Song*

Stephen Fuller

My body now wakes up on its own at 4am
Somehow, transformed from insomniac
To discover the backside of night
And find it as pleasing as Goldilocks
Found the third bed eating the third porridge.
When I talk to the old poet in my journals
Or in files found on my computer that don't
Remember being written, he chuckles at the
Absurdity of the idea of me waking early
To do anything other than take a piss.

My body now wakes up on its own at 4am
The acoustics of this silence are similar
Yet so very different. Waking creatures
Are more for meditations like these than
The beasts that haunt hours that aren't stilled
Inside a heart that hears only its own beating
As it tells tales that ache with longing, with pain
That never really was felt, only misunderstood.
This depth, this texture, this darkness marks
The underside of my eyes just as well, thank you.

My body now wakes up on its own at 4am
Still needing coffee in my oldest possession
Aside from stuffed animals hidden from view:
The coffee mug bought at a convention in college.
My hand still holds the pen, a new lover from Japan,
My sensuous mouth still spills familiar treasures
That makes us fall in love all over again. I adore you.

But now, I feel a presence, like eyes glowing through
A window. I am seen. Seen, my stories take me on
Journeys I didn't even know I wanted to go on.

Eye

Jharna Choudhury

Viral

Upon Waking in a Pandemic

if this be
the end of days
it is not just the world
that has become
unrecognizable
it is me I find
most changed
I thought
I knew myself
oil burning furiously
upon the water
fist raised in defiance
challenging the
heartless gods
only to find myself
instead
drifting rootless
unmoored
in this dark sea
time
barely able to muster
the drive
energy
to stand on raised toes
face tilted toward
the sun
inhale deeply
breathe

Originally published in *As the World Burns: Writers and Artists Reflect on a World Gone Mad*

Pandemic Dreaming
Georgianna Grentzenberg

Pendulum

the pendulum swings
back
and forth
back
and forth
tracing dizzying circles
in white sand
drawing closer
ever closer
to my center
I wait
on a breath
knotted with hope
with anxiety
how close
will its
needle sharp edge
brush my world
how close
will loss
come?
the pendulum swings
back
and forth
back
and forth
back
and forth…

4,087*

knife clenched
in numb fingers
I carve vertical lines
into white plaster
that crumbles
to my touch
effervescent
I notch each loss
deeply into
the walls
a makeshift
memorial
I long for neat
parallel lines
to honor the dead
but my hands
tremble
unsteady

*This poem was written on April 1, 2020 when the total amount of American lives lost to Covid was 4,087. As of September 5, 2023 that number had risen to 1,139,457

Originally published in *As the World Burns: Writers and Artists Reflect on a World Gone Mad*

A Response Poem to 4,087

Stephen Fuller

Hands?
Yours tremble?
Mine shake
like glass
wants broken
into shards
and
crushed under foot
To return to sand
Unmelt me
But first
pick a shard
of me
to help carve
names,
so many…
So many
So many
So many
Wake me from my
nightly nightmare
Screaming, I don't
want it's memory
So many
So many
So many
Pick my shard
off the ground
and carve

Life and Death
Georgianna Grentzenberg

Submersion

waters rose
'round me
so gradually
so soothingly
I barely noticed
when gentle lapping
against bare toes
became insistent
nudging of knees
hips
shoulders
with a feeling
that could be described
relief
I let it gently close
over my head
abandoning myself
to bob
sway
boneless
beneath the surface
from time to time
angel fish
whisper to me
resist
resist
I fight to emerge
filling lungs
painful gasp
after painful gasp
with undiluted broadcasts

eyes assaulted by
unfiltered headlines
ears tormented
by buzz of a million
angry hornets
it does not
take very long
until I again
embrace surrender
drift back into
watery depths
unexpectedly grateful
to find gills
have grown
along my ribs
brightly colored fish
who do not
know the world
of men
entwined in my
seaweed hair
who dart
who play

Originally published in *As the World Burns: Writers and Artists Reflect on a World Gone Mad*

Apocalypse

the world burns
wild
chaotic
flames licking
at my heels
melts amber
encasing me
drop by
precious drop
preferred armor
for fragile sanity
beginning to blur
bubble
fail
primal scream
growing deep
in my gut
barely suppressed
I teeter
one presidential tweet
one revisionist headline
one bigoted Facebook post
away from bursting
supernova
simultaneously
struck by irony
of how protected
how privileged
this life of mine
really is
wearing accident-of-birth

white
female
middle-class skin
with equal parts
grief
shame
self-hatred
relief
I look out
my suburban window
watching mute
while
the world burns. . .

Originally published in *As the World Burns: Writers and Artists Reflect on a World Gone Mad*

Other Voices, Other Rooms

war does not rage
outside these
fragile windows
i lay my head
to sleep
lulled by
privileged safety
of these four
walls of
soothing green
roar of tanks
exploding bombs
mercifully
distant
bellows of rage
of defiance
wails of grief
of terror and
dying whispers
belonging
to other voices
other rooms
this laden night

Stitcher's Elegy

I do not have
walls enough
to hang
the elegies
we stitch
our hands
moving rhythmically
in and out
of stretched cloth
to calm
troubled minds
sooth erratic beating
of heavy hearts
floss flows silken
through pierced eyes
of silver needles
shining light
upon shared humanity
seaming connection
between us
across countless
miles
a dove
emerges

on hooped linen
keens heartbreaking
plea
for peace

Dove (Seek Peace, and Pursue It)

Pattern for peace designed by Aya Rosen and stitched by
Christine E. Ray

Rooms So Still, So Silent

Recombinant Selves

with Marcia J. Weber, Laurie Wise, Kindra M. Austin,
Sarah Doughty, John W. Leys, Allister Nelson, Ward
Clever, OldePunk, Stephen Fuller

We inherit
the wordless cry
of all our former
selves
Christine E. Ray

They layer themselves
upon us
ragged cloaks
of the homeless
dragging
at our heels
Marcia J. Weber

Dusk takes one last breath
swallowing golden specks of us
scattered among the detritus
no light reflects
from such depths
we are the chosen
Laurie Wise

We stumble against starless darkness
searching for one truth
Kindra M. Austin

Layer by layer, I am revealed.
The reflection looking back at me
isn't one I recognize.

Will there be anything
worth remembering,
when I'm gone?
Sarah Doughty

Searching for a candle in the abyss,
a hope to hold onto,
to chalk sweaty palms
tripping a frayed rope.
Tearing tender flesh,
climbing toward salvation
John W. Leys

But the stars have fallen, smashed diamonds
of our shattered images, and the lost cry
who am I? In tune with our hearts.
Allister Nelson

Through telescopes
we focus on a point
All else is irrelevant
From the bottom of a well
our vision is limited
All else is a mystery
Ward Clever

The mysterious property
of my ancestors
the progeny of dusk
I am prodigy or effigy
What I ought to be
or another misstep in
my fragile history
OldePunk

Our former
selves
cry:
Look
their
inheritance!
Stephen Fuller

Bicameral

Georgianna Grentzenberg

Originally published in *But You Don't Look Sick: The Real Life Adventures of Fibro Bitches, Lupus Warriors, and other Superheroes Battling Invisible Illness*

Winter Whites I

I paint
melancholy
on winter white
parchment
the texture
crisped rice
beneath
sable tip
frosted breath
hovers
cloudlike
above
brush strokes
leaving
delicate
shapes
obscured,
unfathomable

Winter Whites II (Paler Shade of Winter)

I long to paint
but this unceasing
palette
of dirty whites
of tired grays
that lurk outside
each window
sucks the rich
marrow
from my bones
whittles my winter-
chilled fingers
into skeletal twigs
silvery bark peeling
clumsy
useless
a cardinal briefly
breaks my
monotonous horizon
a small spot
of vivid crimson
I drink thirstily
with tired eyes
I wonder if
could I render
its flight
on white parchment
or is even my
pigment
my life's blood
grown

too weak
too pale?

Solitary Tree

Jharna Choudhury

Stars Slip Through My Hands

rendered transparent
a ghost in my own life
my heart
an empty room
so still
so quiet
it hurts
saltwater
tracing facial curves
feel of fingertips
resting idle
on plastic keys
only tangible reminder
that I am made
of more than
mist
of memory
all I value
slips out
of my grip
hands still
lacking the agility
the strength
to catch the stars
as they slip from my sky

I am a Ghost

Georgianna Grentzenberg

A Room So Still and Silent It Hurts: A Collaboration of Warriors

with Rachel Finch, Rana Kelly, Kindra M. Austin, Sarah Doughty, Eric Syrdal, Ward Clever, Marcia J. Weber, Dom Wynette, Aakriti Kuntal, Lois Linkens, Laurie Wise, OldePunk, and Nathan McCool

in a room so still and silent
that it hurts
stark white walls
razor sharp edges
etch my soul
draw blood
that drips slowly
soundlessly
from my mouth
Christine Ray

I am trapped
like a fly in amber
Time stands still
The air is thick
Holds me motionless
in this prison cell
I feel vibration
A silent scream building
from my depths
Rachel Finch

Barricaded, her aura stifles
in the quiet.
Walls closing in, silence
penetrating.
Her mind internally

burning, blistering.
His voice a faint echo,
worlds away.

I tell them they're lying,
the monsters that cling
to the lobes and whorls
of my ears.
They laugh and go on.
I pull the covers up
to my chin and let them in again
until the tears are spent
and still,
they never repent.
Get thee behind me,
but I always look back
waiting on them to pounce.
Rana Kelly

In a room so still, I draw mental images.
Shovelfuls of dirt are tossed and splayed;
loose earth lands with a dead sound
upon my ridiculous casket.
The images play in a loop like
spliced film—a silent movie.
Kindra M. Austin

These bones have grown
weak and weary, while the rest
of the world has gone
dark and gray. Over time,
they've become more
than I can handle.
More than I can live with.
And these burdens I carry

are mine alone. No one
deserves to hold them
on their shoulders.
Which is why I'll take them
with me. After the music
stops playing.
Sarah Doughty

In a room so still
I hear echoes of a former life
I hear the twisting and creaking
of this thread I hang from
Knotted and frayed it
binds my heart
in pieces that have shattered
So many times they no longer
fit together
and their edges are so razor sharp
They cut me to ribbons
to remember what I once was
Eric Syrdal

I scream
I lost myself
The echoes dont come back
Ragged and raw, my chords vibrate
revealing nothing from my insides
My voice swallowed up by the crowd
My inner voice silenced
I have become the echoes
Ward Clever

in the silence
my shame shrieks torment
a piercing the walls drill
into my brain

the ceiling salivates venom
it licks the stiffness
from my spine
the floor nauseates me
as it breathes
rank sour breath
of the unlovable, whose caries
grew unfettered in an unkissed mouth
I shrink, a knotted ball,
from the reverberating stench,
the putrefying death knell
inverted, I am a tunnel
from which no light escapes
there is only the abject crawling
of my soul, face down
in the sewage
of my failed spirit
Marcia J. Weber

I hate this fucking room…
I hate being consumed with my doom…
As I sit here, looking at my shattered reflection in the perfect mirror
all I am forever reminded of,
is what I almost was…
Why can I not seem to get back on track?
All that was an almost happy life has gone to pure shit..
blinded by the bright light at the end of the dark tunnel…
I should follow it…
Even if it means I am dead forever, and I can't come back…
Even if it makes me weak…
I am just tired of being strong…
Maybe even tired of holding on…
There has to be another side..

A place where I can freely roam,
a place where I don't have to hide…
Reality is overwhelming…
This room is so silent…that it fucking hurts
my head is full of too many traumatic memories…
I am running out of do-over's at this point…
I have done everything to release
The only time I hear that I am good enough…
is after I please a nobody…so I am just a good fuck…
I don't believe in me anymore… I am out of good luck…
I need to be free from life… from turmoil…
I need to be free from being me…
I hate being stuck…
Dom Wynette

Long hands, circumcision of thought,
flailing flesh, fish sucking the rotten sea
The window breast is now red from approach
We hang there, we do
the captivity of bleached air is like nothing else
the death sentence of genes
Godless children of a different race
Our hearts are split and our brains feverish
slowly descending, soaked head to toe
into songs that contain only air
I twist the lock, your twisted face, a warped kite
Floating across ceilings,
You have decided to spread
a smile wide as the day, light up the dim structure of your face
Like blow torches growing mad above the taste of ashes
You have decided to smile
this one last time
And the ceiling watches,
its silence repulsive

And the walls judge,
their jabber exhausting
Men like to slaughter what they don't understand
Common cold doesn't dictate cancer
And neither mood nor perspective is the predecessor of mental
sickness
The floor watches,
stained in a lovely red
The only living thing now
is you
and you, you bleed
Upwards into a cerulean sky
Aakriti Kuntal (Warped Kites)

i don't belong here.
i stick out like a black sheep in a field of white,
a pebble strung on a thread of pearls.
oh, that piece would be so fetching
with pearls alone,
and i am sure the shepherd grows weary of the sight of me.
Lois Linkens

The anguish of aliveness
No one wins
Sterile, self-defeating
Shrouded in intense sensitivity
Silence, secrets, sadness, solitude
A welcomed stillness
Such sweet solace
The weight begins to lift
A final gift
Believe
There is a peace
in release

A freedom beyond
this relentless realm
A breakable bond
from devils and demons
Laurie Wise

The melodies are
my legacy
I've won some battles
but I am losing the war
choose not to remember
my last act
but all of the victories
that came before
as a samurai chooses
death over dishonor
my seppuku is the solution
to stop the coming horror
the monster with my smile
I know that my absence
will fill a room so still
it hurts but better
still than to see the world
I love burn with my
dark needs
OldePunk

You know when I'm there, after all the blood,
after all my ghost begin to break up and
dissipate like early morning radio chatter,
after the loss
of every god damn thing I've ever loved,
I can tell you that I earned the cognizance
that this was never a room.
Rooms have an exit, but there is no re-entry

into what my life used to be.
It's a black hole, and on the other side
there is a universe of all dead bodies.
So if I dissect myself,
if I show you all my organs that could never
have managed to hold this cancer,
if I do it here at the altar of all my great
rewards…
I just want you to know I've reached the
event horizon.
But here I do not struggle, I strive. I still
yearn to be a good man. Wish that my
heart would become supermassive,
and strong enough to maybe release
one singular ray of light into all this space.
Set one lone kite free of gravity.

If I fall through the hole and I'm never seen again,
I want you to remember I wasn't a coward.
I was the thing that withstood longer than
all else.
Because nothing can be here if it still
has a world to belong to.
And if you don't understand that, in a way
I hope you never do.
But if you never saw my light, if I gave in
before it could break through
I'm sorry.
It's not because I didn't try.
So live or die,
Be free or killed by this monster of my mind,
I did the very best that I could.
Nathan McCool

One Night I Dreamed...

Georgianna Grentzenberg

Unwritten

the suicide note
she did not leave
left a faint imprint
on the wooden table
where they would sit and talk
over cups of milky coffee
the suicide note
she did not leave
rang like silence in his ears
the suicide note
she did not leave
burned itself onto his retinas
he feared the afterimage
was permanent
the suicide note
she did not leave
did not list
13 reasons why
he understood only
that the starless darkness
she was drowning in
had become so thick
so viscous
so acidic

that it had eaten all light
and she could no longer see
how he glowed
whenever she was near

*'Unwritten' was inspired by the spoken word poem 'Phases' by
Kevin Kantor & Sienna Burnett*

A Song with Many Voices: All the Lonely People
with Sarah Doughty, Kindra M. Austin, Laurie Wise,
Basiliké Pappa, John W. Leys, Michael Erickson, Ward
Clever, OldePunk, Marcia J. Weber, Lois Linkens, Devika
Mathur, and Stephen Fuller

I have always been here, among the lonely people. Despite
having people around me, my battles exist within my head and
body. To you, I may look normal, but on the inside is a scene
entirely different. My constant companions are sadness,
frustration, exhaustion — even a fortified fortress to shield me
from what the world has and could continue to do to me. Those
walls isolate me from my family. The shadows are filled with
creatures that know how to hurt me if I move too close. So, you
see, I am one of the lonely people. But
I am not alone.
Sarah Doughty

All the Lonely People—
they converge,
invisible at intersections
of Life and Death,
strangely untouched by hands of those
simpatico.
How can it be that so many similar
do exist while lost
to one another?
All the Lonely People—
they are unalone, and yet
desperately segregated;
misinterpretations
made by cold analyses
appease

the masses,
give excuses to
maintain blindness.
Kindra M. Austin

All the lonely people
We hide
In shadows
Contemplating reason
Bleeding truth
Brutality and madness
Clinging to singing
Bones of what used to be
Combing catacombs
In search of slightest light
And notes of hope
Scribbled on worn script
A story of happy endings
Dangling on threatening thread
Of human connection
Just out of reach
Contradictory condition
Unaccompanied euphony
Love song for the lonely
Laurie Wise

Sometimes this house like walls within,
life angel-blind or saint-sedated.
Wearing madness as a hat,
phrasing themselves into escapes,
sunken flames and the mirror broken,
every memory drained of wonder,
the lonely people:
afraid that birth may be repeated.
Basiliké Pappa

All the lonely people
Sleep waking dark streets
Under overcast skies,
Red rimmed eyes
And sepia toned faces
Singing songs no one will hear,
Writing poems no one will read,
Born with hope and potential
Dying with nothing but a name,
Buried in a box
Covered with loose dirt
And half hearted prayers.
No one was saved.
John W. Leys

All the lonely people,
Where do we all belong?
With masks of happiness concealing our fears,
We pass others by.
Looking for meaning between echoing footfalls,
Where emptiness only lies.
Oh how I wish I could remove this mask,
And show others how I feel.
For lonely people need more than just objects and things,
Connection, understanding, and a listening ear.
We belong to each other from beginning to end,
We all share similar fears.
All these lonely people,
Where do we all belong?
Michael Erickson

Look at the lonely
Making connections with other invisible friends
It never ends
Look in the mirror

They cannot see eye to eye with their reflection's gaze
Live in a daze
The image in the mirror
What makes you feel alive??
All the lonely people
Belong to the same tribe
Ward Clever

A name for the beetles
to eat along with the flowers
at my lone grave
buried on a hill
under a chill
and no one came
I know now where
the alone belong
but I could have been saved
by a song
that nobody sang
look at all the lonely people
you should know that it's
all wrong
OldePunk

all the lonely people
croon their heartbroken harmonies
stretch aching arms
across unspoken chasms
estranged
in disconsolate silences.
yearning for connection
they swaddle themselves
in quilts of embroidered sorrows,
every painstaking stitch
a shimmering titanium shield.

all the lonely people
asphyxiate
on swallowed inarticulations
while their marrows vibrate
— hummed exhalations—
with universal laments.
Marcia J. Weber

we fear it,
the yellow beast in Prufrock's alley,
when the grimy backstreets
of nobody's business will teem with life.
the moon rises
and in her pearly face i see myself,
orange street lamps spill across her glow,
leaving
watery damage,
green fingers and old jewelry,
deadened with use.
all the lonely people—
they fill up on earth and sky.
Lois Linkens

To see sanguine ropes of dirt and mollusk
we walk under the skins of disgust, often choking
Slumping, sliding under the caskets of Coffins
Biting the threads of skulls, breathing the sands of hope
We have a thumping noise, striking our iris and hands
Shivers and cold Noises.
Filling the brim of the Planet with liquids and milk
we march towards our home.
All the lonely people,

We exist still, under the cleft of your chins,
under the blue sonograms,
under the pits and pits.
We are the lonely people
Devika Mathur

                    Arrows and stones: a child's song
                         protects the fragile boy
                       from all who want to paint him
                          as if he were as blank as Locke
                    as if he just arrived on the cul-de-sac
                       that morning for the first time:
                                    He had not.
                          He was there the day before.
                    He had been there days before that
                          and so on… like a hall of mirrors
                    reflecting him back and forth, forever,
                                    he'd been there.
                          Now, though, now,
                               they see him cry
                          and think: AHA! A fete!
          "On him, I can paint all the shades of my pain,"
          as if the color under his skin wasn't on the spectrum.
                                    Stephen Fuller

all the lonely people
where do we all belong?
trapped behind sheets of ice
our voices whisper
our heartbeats slow
our fingers too stiff
too unpracticed
to break through our walls to reach out
and touch
those technicolor people

who blaze bright before our starved eyes
who somehow laugh
love
and live without reservation
what do they know
that we don't?
we long to gather their light
their warmth
cradle it to our frozen chests
feed the ember that flickers there
make it smolder
make it burn
until our desperate cries of
I am!
finally cuts through the night
like a knife
Christine E. Ray

Leakage
Jharna Choudhury

Roads of Broken Glass

there are nights
breathing
feels like crawling
along a road
of dirt
of stone
of broken glass
embedding itself raggedly
into flesh
leaving bloody handprints
smudged knee smears
in my wake
my sky too low
for standing
no place of comfort
no place to rest
weary bones
pierced skin

Off the Rails

Elijah R. Carney

Unheard Incantations

with Kindra M. Austin, Marcia J. Weber, John W. Leys,
Michael Erickson, Laurie Wise, Lois Linkens, Sarah
Doughty, and Stephen Fuller

The words we cannot say
Will be wept
Into silence between us
Christine E. Ray

> Breathe deep, dear love;
> Be still with me
> Listen to my heartstrings
> A song meant just for you
> *Kindra M. Austin*

Each tear
An eloquent elegy
To tortured truths
Marcia J. Weber

> Each note played
> On a hand carved lute
> Strung with strips
> Of my soul
> *John W. Leys*

Your breathless aura
Beats in time
Undulating ululation
With my exhaled psyche
Marcia J. Weber

> Intertwined, tangled,
> Unified: whole
> Healed.

John W. Leys

Yet with hearts torn open
Bleeding out the notes of our song
You turned from me
Michael Erickson

I am fire
Drowning
In desire
Weep
I beg
Save me
Laurie Wise

Fetch me an instrument,
For the untrained ear
Is soothed by that
Which it cannot comprehend.
Lois Linkens

Not everything is black and white.
For even the eclipsed moon
Is not without a little light.
Sarah Doughty

Whispers through the distance
I remember
As you reach for my hand
My heart
Christine E. Ray

Our words
Still
Bleeding
Drip like fire
Into embers

Wanting back
Their flame.
Stephen Fuller

The words we cannot say
Will be wept
Into silence between us
Christine E. Ray

Sparse

Elijah R. Carney

Queue the Music
with Stephen Fuller

applause
fills my ears like
gin in my glass
accolades for how well
I convey pain
others' consume.
I am their proxy
their stand-in
these words
tears,
blood
I give
tiny pins
that prick
nerves like
strings
tying up
this human condition
I am grateful
appreciative
for the shot
at the main stage
the time you give
me to speak for
the lonely
the voiceless
the desperate
the crowd
praises my performance

my art
feeling too much
music
fades
me
out
this fancy
red carpet
dress returns
to an empty
dressing room
to drink the gin
alone

#

My Lonely Seasons Pass
with Stephen Fuller

The days blend, one into the other,
waking naked into the world, I stare
into a meaningless blur trying for
definition with a shave and makeup
armor to protect from soulless work
seeping inside these walls to steal
what remains of my fight. I sleep
empty in bed, cold featureless sheets
cover my flesh, only virgin pillows
wrapped in white, offering contours.
Loneliness like a season failing passage.

Tongue Tied

Speak

there is an art
to talking everything
about what is nothing
while saying nothing
about what is
everything
to paint
convincing illusions
of intimacy
candor
that successfully deflect
the curious eye
while frantically
stuffing down
the secrets that
chew at your gut
the poison of shame
corroding your veins
the self-blame
you inhale daily
into your lungs
believing that nothing
is as deadly
as dangerous
as devastating
as your truth

Struck Mute

I am
a woman
built
of words
it is not
natural
comfortable
intuitive
for me
to tie
my tongue
tightly
to choose
silence
to be mute
to opt for
discretion
over
valor
but you yank
syllables
from my
mouth
tie them
into knots
twist them
into
unrecognizable
shapes
hone sharp edges
they did not

originally
contain
accuse them
of drawing
blood

Masked

Jharna Choudhury

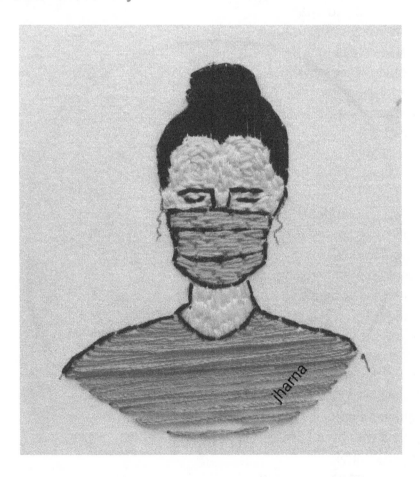

Darker objects

poetry is oft
written
by those who
love too
much
too freely
hearts splayed open
on sterile dissection trays
cool stainless pins
trapping vulnerable
fluttering edges
i am a darker
object
I fear I love
too little
too miserly
my specimen heart
muffled below
weighted blankets
fingers absently rolling
small plastic beads
that dwell
below cheerful
cotton covers
hiding the graveyard
that fills
right ventricle
ghosts who haunt the left
atriums full of
cobweb-draped skeletons
loss

unresolved grief
pump through
veins
arteries
thick
black &
sticky

Locked
Elijah R. Carney

I've Got New Rules

I measure time
stitch by
careful stitch
my needle
smoothly gliding
through
the fabric
rhythmic
measured
the threads
weaving
a kind of
peace
with each
neat x
placed
I measure meaning
syllable by
painstaking
syllable
my blood
of ink
alternately
rushing
stumbling
seizing
a breath
such deep
sacred breath
exhaled
with each

word
wrestled
free

Convergence in Aqua, Black and Green
Designed, pieced, and quilted by Christine E. Ray

Are You Fucking New Here?

with Kristiana Reed, Allister Nelson, Marcia J. Weber, Iulia
Halatz, Lois Linkens, Sarah Doughty, and Kindra M.
Austin
A Weyward Sisters Collaboration

you dropped by today
dissected my verse
thoughtfully pointed out
all the ways I could
smooth out my edges
improve flow
to slide more gently past
your discerning eyes
you must be fucking new here
if you think
I was asking for it
not a fan of unsolicited advice
my "friend"
I like my truth
raw
bloody
with a hint of lemon for acidity
that stings going down
Christine E. Ray

Oh, hello,
I didn't see you there
although I can already tell you like to stare,
as if it is your obligation
to females everywhere.
And everywhere you seem to be.
You're the type who lingers in keyboards,

assaulting our letters
with ones you would never dare to speak.
You're the type who visits galleries just to sigh,
point out the vulvas in the petals
and tut at a landscape you've never visited.
You're the type who slumps way down in the theatre,
feigning sleep during her monologue
because it is 'feminist and shit', and yet
she'll be the only one on your mind
when you reach down tonight.
Oh, how do I know this?
Why, because you always come back for more.
For more of my letters, pretty letters,
your coeliac stomach cannot wait to reject.

Kristiana Reed

You stab me with a misplaced comma's edge,
expect me to bleed ink, but I blossom gold
leaf, like pages of a holy tome, and your
lines of prose crackle in my burning gale.
I am more word than woman, you see
and I am truth, your haunting just ghost
of all those who said no, who pushed me
down stairs of paragraphs, but I got grit,
I grew wings of paper, from you I fly.

Allister Nelson

hey you there –
with the pursed lips
and furrowed brow
click-clacking
your studied
critical analysis
of these driblets
of my life's blood.

135

you must be fucking new here
if you mistake
the penning
of my soul
upon the page
as a request
for literary critique.
this, here
is the juice of my carotid
scrawled with fingertips
as I apply
tourniquet and poultice.
your worded attempts
to package my agony
into neat and tidy
boxes
are ill-advised salt flakes
poured into my wounds.
Marcia J. Weber

Soft upon the scene
He entered
Mushy odorless rambling
Entailed:
"Darling, how are you faring?
Your words are dancing in my soul
Your star shines upon my dreams."
going after me
Feeling my every words' step
With a presumptuous club
White and black penned music
That clawed silence to my ears:

"You are the brightest…
Fade away, you heartless beast!"
Iulia Halatz

i picked up my pen and out came all of me.
it poured and poured,
filling space with untrained words
sharp love, bent feelings,
a keenness breathed without judgement,
ink balled with mercy
into something true of me.
but you sat, held your cup,
watched it spill.
you put it in your cabinet
with a yellow note.
i would those curling lips
might taste the poison in the teacup
between your eyes;
that is where the horror really lies.

Lois Linkens

You must be new here, because tact and common decency seem lost on you. You see, it is not okay to call a woman by any other name than the one she has given — so don't call me Baby and I won't call you Tiny. It is not okay to insert yourself in my life and assume I need your sage advice— if I want to know, I will ask. Do not presume to know what I am thinking, or what my heart is trying to say— because you can be damn sure that if I wrote the words, I meant each and every one of them. I'm not perfect, and I never claimed to be, but I don't need a lecture on semantics or grammar — I've had more than enough schooling and experience to know

my own mind. But, if you really are new here, remember this one simple rule: if you don't have something nice to say, don't say anything
at all.
Sarah Doughty

You enter my house and
manhandle my verse. You
wonder why my
heart spurts crimson with
every heavy beat—
pressure me for information.
Why so mocking?
Why so angry?
Why the foul language? Bitch,
you must be fucking new here
if you expect an
explanation.
Cos I don't answer stupid
questions.
Grow a brain, and
get a clue.
Kindra M. Austin

Originally published by the *Sudden Denouement Literary Collective*

Crabby

Elijah R. Carney

Tenterhooks

Monday Morning Mantra

it's just pain
it's just pain

fervent mantra
echoing in my
brain
knuckles fisted white
upon cane's
smooth purple handle
muscles
tendons
resisting
stretching
tearing
shrieking
from ball
and socket
joint
vertebrae
compressed tight
rub against
each other
in annoyance
grating upon
each other's
nerves
I list drunkenly
to the right
a sailor who has
lost sea legs

tower with
crumbling
foundation
I take another
stagger step

it's just pain
it's just pain

Bones of Pain

Georgianna Grentzenberg

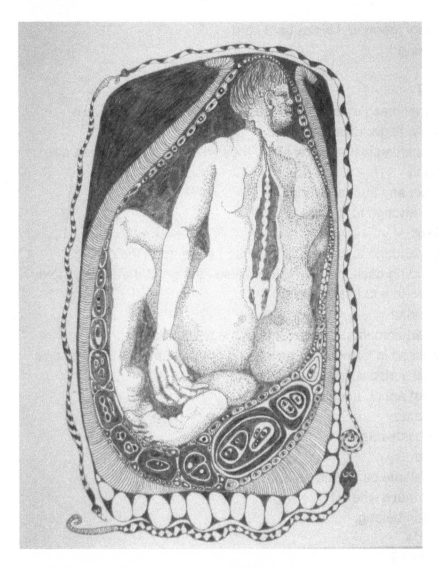

Originally published in *But You Don't Look Sick: The Real Life Adventures of Fibro Bitches, Lupus Warriors, and other Superheroes Battling Invisible Illness*

Entropy
with Kindra M. Austin

Every morning, I wake up. I keep
waking
up.
And
sometimes I'm angry at my opened eyes, cos sometimes
brittle fingernails
scratching inside of my skull, they split and rip and bleed and
blood
leaks and shorts my circuits.
Not enough to kill me
dead,
just enough to kill my will. And so I stare up at the ceiling,
counting back the years, the weeks, the goddamned days I've
given in and left myself to
dreadful
entertainments. Circus tents of made up horrors
dressed in homemade gore—red corn syrup and hot dogs and
mushy elbow macaroni.
What am I? Incubator for the fly.
bzzzzzz
I am infestation,
lying.
Nighttime calls, and so I answer,
cos that's where I
fuckin belong.
Inside
black ink

sky—where nerve endings scream in silence of
outer space.
Kindra M. Austin

Every morning, I wake up. I keep
waking
up,
fighting cobwebs of nightmares that cling to my brain
like black taffy.
My bed covers a cotton shroud, moldering around heavy limbs.
The smell of decay and musty lavender fill my nose, make me
retch,
remind me that I'm rotting from the inside in this weak vessel of
flesh.
The sunlight creeping under the blinds is acid that burns my
eyes.
I close my lids tightly, seeking escape from the awaiting nothing,
but even my ghosts have retreated for the day;
and I'm left with nothing but long hours I no longer
have the energy to fill.
What am I? An empty husk of a woman.
A corpse with a pulse,
who forgot to fall.
Nighttime calls, and so I answer
sleep's promise of oblivion.
The electric sheep I try to count
sting me like jellyfish,
leave weeping blisters on my soul
before melting into the obsidian.
Christine E. Ray

Originally published in *But You Don't Look Sick: The Real Life Adventures
of Fibro Bitches, Lupus Warriors, and other Superheroes Battling Invisible
Illness*

147

Ceramic Tile, Sea

Georgianna Grentzenberg

Byte

hyper-
focus
is an art
I slip into
words
into screen
until
I am
nothing…
nothing
but blinking
cursor
nothing
but task
decoded
into nibbles
into bytes
I swim free
I dread
interruption
disruption
yanks me rudely
violently
back
into
body
no longer
able
to block out
to ignore
this wrecked

vessel
excruciatingly
aware
full bladder
burning thirst
unending
ache
in every
minute
joint
ceaseless
pain

Shoulds

I should
brand myself
a failure
self-flagellate
for failing to meet
expectations
of those
who wear
white coats
shiny stethoscopes
draped casually
around necks
I should let
their stern eyes
their nonverbal—
but surprisingly loud—
condemnation of
my parenting
echo through my mind
but right now
I am just
too fatigued
just too
damn tired
to bathe
in their judgment
wallow in expected
self-hatred
too worn
from chronic illness
chronic pain

that tightly fitted
jumpsuit of
hair and barbed
wire
even
for that

Pins and Needles

thunder has been rumbling for the last few weeks
under my skin
hair standing up on the back of my neck
my arms
a storm has been brewing
I am edgy, uncomfortable
reality keeps twisting into a Dali landscape
I keep ending up in the Lost & Found bin
voiceless
disoriented
unable to account for all my minutes
all my hours
they say that our brains are remarkable at protecting us from
trauma
from what we are not ready to consciously face
my brain and I are having a difference of opinion on just how
ready
I am for sensoroma film clips to come bubbling up to my surface
right now
I remember…
keeps echoing in my head
I don't know that
I really want to remember any
more than I already do
I hope to find humor yet about it happening
during the middle of an acupuncture treatment
apparently, reception is pretty good on the
Flashback Channel with needles penetrating my skin
maybe next time I'll skip the silver foil blanket…

Shattered Mirror

woke up wrong side of the bed
all pins
and needles
and porcupine quills
thunder and lightning
brewing under my skin
as throbbing nerves
at the base of my spine
spread tendrils
of electricity
to my fingers and toes
until I want to scream
my hands itching
to throw the lamp
at my mirrored reflection
watch the glass
fall in beautiful shards
as it unleashes the monster
calling me
from the other side
welcome her warmly into my arms
we shall twirl
round and round
until we are a blur
until our feet bleed
boundaries dissolve
and we finally
become almost one

heads thrown back
in reckless laughter
wicked delight
time to breathe fire

Mask, Venice
Jharna Choudhury

Dancing at the Edge of the Cliff

lulled into a false sense of
pharmacological security
I forget
how close
I hover to the abyss

caught unaware by how stealthily
darkness can slither back to the surface
swirling sinuously around my ankles
wrists
gray smoke to weight manacles
in what feels like an instant

darkness triumphs rapidly
transforming me
into something
other

mouth lengthening into beak
I squawk indignantly in protest
as skin sprouts
razer-sharp quills
feet become claws
deeply scratching the floor

fingers stretch into talons
tipped with steel
that I use to rip myself
to tatters
remove
my own heart

before biting into it
with
teeth made fangs
till blood hotly runs
down my chin

Rage Against the Machine

We Cannot Look Away: Not another seventeen, not another One

with **Devereaux Frazier, Basiliké Pappa, Eric Syrdal, Nicholas Gagnier, Megha Sood, Sarah Doughty, Kindra M. Austin, Michael Erickson, Stephen Fuller, and John W. Leys**

Just another day
just another town
bullet perforated backpacks
spilling loose-leaf lined paper, textbooks
onto blood stained sidewalks
helicopters hovering
to give us the birds eye view
I tried to avert my eyes
out of respect for the dead
the injured
but I could not look away
Christine Ray

Even though I should
Because I am ashamed
At the bullets that rain
At the bullet point pain
Etched in their faces, rivulets in their eyes
They were just children, stolen from their time
Not forgotten in these lines
But to their parents and loved ones
It's a void they'll never fill, and it shouldn't
Lives shredded and ruined
17 times we've gotten the chance to do better
and for the 18th, we blew it
Just like those children who looked at their killer

Their killer is not Nikolas
The Killer is you
Devereaux Frazier

Seventeen blossoms
seventeen blinks of an eye
seventeen bullets in the body of spring
and those left behind
food to flashback phobias
memory outbursts
numbing
Spring won't be coming
in a town far away
in a country across the sea
right next to me
Basiliké Pappa

Running
Running for class president
Running for the Varsity Football Team
Running to get in line for a movie they can't wait to see
Running to embrace someone they love
Running and laughing with siblings or friends
Running to get to the dance floor before their favorite song ends
Running for exercise
Running for fun
They should never be running from the thunder of a gun
We're destroying our future for profit and gain
while they run for their lives
and we're left with questions and pain
Eric Syrdal

Look away, little bird.
The sky has adjourned, rejecting your flight path
well into wrath.
hell hath no fury like the anger turned apathy, semi-automatic
rhapsody that plays on
the overhead speaker that once freed us
from maths.
It doesn't add up, the physics, social studies, introduction to
business, life and
death 101.
Nothing could prepare us for the words we don't have.
Nicholas Gagnier

Lives swung into darkness
and voices numbed
Eyes losing hope
Blood on the hands, soul
screams and tears everywhere
Deafening silence of the death
and roaring sound of the violence
life stripped of its happiness
and tears losing the feeling
Yet again, My heart is hopeful
Lips in unison with the prayers
Trying to calm myself down
Thinking It won't happen again
But deep down inside
I know we all are living in denial.
Megha Sood

Spare me your
thoughts and prayers.
Spare me your
people-kill-people babble.
Seventeen more names

added to a statistic
that will never be used.
So, by all means,
let's keep sending
millions of dollars a year
to powerful people
in exchange for turning
a blind eye.
Proving over and over again
that dollars mean more
than lives.
Sarah Doughty

Seventeen more reasons we grieve.
Seventeen more reasons we're
broken as a nation.
Seventeen more reasons we must
rise up
a giant against apathy, and
negligence—
willful ignorance.
Destroy the dissidence.
End the agenda of greed.
Our freedoms are not free—
seventeen more innocent souls sacrificed.
Kindra M. Austin

True horror has unfolded,
We watch on glowing screens of disbelief.
With the voices of innocents ringing in our ears,
Fingers swipe it all away.
As others moved on with their day,
I could not look away.
Grief, pain, disbelief,
All right there, before our eyes.

164

Yet one headline replaces the next,
That gut wrenching sadness suddenly replaced.
As the topic changes to something else,
I could not look away.
Where is our humanity,
I ask as society moves on from this butchered elephant in the
room.
Can't we just stop and think,
Acknowledge the death, the suffering, the wrongness.
Another day will come and go, setting on our community,
We cannot look away.
Doomed to repeat this dreadful fate,
We need to choose to change.
Insanity is as insanity always does,
As we continue to place ammunition with malignant intent.
What can I do, the individual, the lone soul, this:
I will not look away.
Michael Erickson

We
Only
Have ourselves
To blame for this
Again and again
An unsolved tragedy
We must hold ourselves to task
For every death. Every child
Like spent shells fallen to the ground
Souls adrift to haunt those who do not act –
Who do not act again and again and again
I cannot look away again, again, again
Again
Again
Again

Again
Again, again, again, again, I cannot look away, not again.
Stephen Fuller

I cannot look away
From the train wreck shit show
This country has become,
Where cash in a senator's pocket
Outweighs the blood of our children,
Where losing your 'right' to own an assault rifle
Is more an abomination
Than Children being murdered in school
Than human beings dying at a concert in Vegas
Than parents burying their babies.
The blood on your hands will not wash away.
I'm with you in Parkland!
Where kids call presidents out on their bullshit.
I'm with you in Parkland!
Where they won't let hypocrites hide.
I'm with you in Parkland!
Where they call BS on the lies.
I'm with you in Parkland!
John W. Leys

Howling

Elijah R. Carney

The Madness of Crowds
Parkland, February 14, 2018

the streets run red
with the blood
of innocents
deemed acceptable
collateral damage
in an uncivil war
where corporations
and fetuses
enjoy more rights
more protections
than living children
who remain caught
in the crosshairs
their transparent packs
carried on slight shoulders
heavy with the weight
of our future
stains from the latest
massacre scrubbed from
the asphalt
barely dry
before the NRA waves the
photoshopped
photochopped
Bill of Rights
in one hand
as they pass out
AR-15s loaded
with venom
and vitriol

with the other
while well-dressed politicians
walk on stealthy feet
whisper softly
to aim at the cattle chutes
students now wait in
before walking
single-file through
metal detectors
incredulous and disgusted
when they are told
that this will make them "safe"

The Wages of War

Georgianna Grentzenberg

With Clenched Fists, I Rage

with John W. Leys, Deveraux Frazier, Marcia J. Weber,
Megha Sood, Stephen Fuller, and Candice Louisa Daquin

I chew on my rage
breaking teeth
on its rock candy
hard edges
I resist
base reflex
to swallow these
jagged shards whole
instead
spitting blood
and shrapnel
hard
into
the unrelenting soil
of injustice
Christine E. Ray

My fist clenches unconsciously,
Noticing only when my knuckles pop.
They say peace and love
Will win the day,
While I'm possessed
By the spirit of Elijah,
Raining down fire,
Divine justice, and rage,
Filled with the desire
To bludgeon bigotry
With a baseball bat.
John W. Leys

Wretched causeway
Flotsam upon my eye
I stare into the mist in wonder
Will the serpent ever arise
Show me your face, foul beast
You tinker and toy with mortal men
Spewing hatred and obscenities with forked tongues
Crucifying anyone who stands firm against them
Justice beckons their immortal fear
Wielding the rocks, I guide my hands
Betwixt the evil and the cowardly
Is I
Neither master nor slave
But a watcher
Rising on invisible stream of energy
Deveraux Frazier

I gnash my teeth
flinted in angst
to razors edges
ripping the jugular
out o' malignant lies

remind me Maya
soulful and wise
again and again
how heads held high
above that filth
We rise
Marcia J. Weber

My rage coursing through my veins
with clenched fists
enraged as the lava
birthing the mountains

in the blink of an eye,
the seething anger
pulsating in every
throbbing vein
of mine,
my whole existence
shivers and whimpers
at the mere sight
of this atrocity,
those mendacious protectors
holding reins to this
monstrous political toxicity
Megha Sood

Beware
I am a drop of water
Contagious hydrophilic rage
Slipping into the crack
In your granite
Waiting for Winter
Stephen Fuller

ends begin when good people
do nothing
beginnings eat the rot
spit out bad seeds
leave them to bloom
in Covid sunlight
devoid of laughter
see what comes? Of
chewed intent and
hope on hock?
Candice Louisa Daquin

Originally published on *Heretics, Lovers, and Madmen*

Ceramic Tile, Snake
Georgianna Grentzenberg

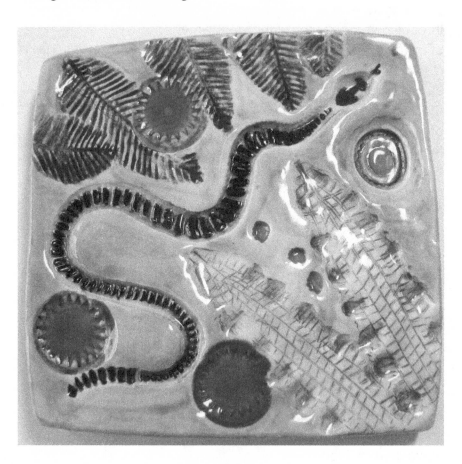

October 26, 2020

I am living
on caffeine
and anxiety
my diet nutrient-
and comfort-
poor
occasional
sips of hope
curdle instantly
against inflamed walls
of my leaky gut
hands pressed
tightly to my
abdomen
I fight to contain
the acid wash
of my rage
grief
dread
I am living
disability check to
disability check
furtively
shoulders hunched
to shield
my pain
fatigue
shame
what will
happen
to me-

and others
like me-
when we are caught
by the unblinking eyes
of proud boys
and woman of praise
judged lacking
unworthy
useless
in this brave
new world?

Flags

I toss and turn
despite closed lids
images etch onto my corneas
of your torches, your flags
symbols of hate
it is the confidence
pride
with which you carry these symbols
that truly haunts me
no need to hide your identity
in this New America
led by madmen
who value nothing but themselves
content to let
this country burn
as long as egos remain stroked
as long as they can feed off power
chaos
like succubi
until bellies are full
but we forget
they are insatiable
you feel comfortable
justified
to openly express
your hate
your outrage
about all you believe
you have lost
been denied
the war the history books declared over

158 years ago
still rages in your heart
simmered and stewed across generations
you raise your hand in Nazi salute
believing your time
has finally come
in this cultural war
you deem holy
I am awake now
hair standing up on my arms
dis-ease gnawing at my belly
chilled to the bone

Cannon
Elijah R. Carney

Faith Don't Lie
with S.K. Nicholas

Before you, the days blended one into another, each one as empty as the day before. Hell on earth. A month of Sundays, forced to my bare bloody knees onto the cold, hard stone floor by a congregation of pious sleepwalkers, of judgmental sheep. You've met their kind. The ones who can't see. The ones who can't feel. The ones who worship their shiny toys like idols and pray at the twin altars of willful ignorance and empty contentment. They pointed their fingers at me, sewed a red letter on my chest, called me a heretic for wanting more. For declaring you a true prophet.

My faith don't lie, so why should yours? At times like these I feel both dead and alive, and this is how I get my kicks. The knife I twist brings with it the lips of those I wish to kiss above all else. May they kiss me under and may the blade take me to another plateau so I can be at one with God, far from those who resemble what I wish never to resemble. Too many days pissed away. Too many hours left hanging by a thread. Just too much time pretending those wrapped in flesh and sin were like me, but they never were, and neither are you. You know it. I can see it in your eyes. Can feel it when you cry as your world comes tumbling down because the faith you seek is in them and not within.

You baptized me in the woods with the wine and the words of burning truth that bled from your mouth. Told me to dig my fingers deep in the rich earth, feel the hum of life all around us. As the bonfire blazed, you molded the shadows and revealed the secrets of your death and resurrection to my open eyes. I could hear the copper sing in your blood. Taste your holiness on my tongue. I

179

was filled with the crimson gold light of the spirit deep in my marrow. I knew the excruciating glory of rebirth.

My faith don't lie, so why should yours? They spit at the sky and claim the rain falls only on them. Them and their desperate need for affection never giving so much as a thoughtful ear in return. They see shapes while we observe miracles. They hear noise while we hear songs as old as the universe. Yet all they do is try convincing us the magic in our bones is mere illusion. That what we've got to give don't mean shit. But we know that's not true. We've known right from the start. It's in our hearts and these visions that push us further away, but if we've got each other, the more adrift we become the better. So take my hand. Take it now and let's find a beautiful place to get lost.

We turn our backs to the unbelievers, with their deaf ears and eyes that choose not to see. It is not our work to proselytize to the masses. We will minister to ones like us, who cannot settle for the stale, tasteless bread, the white picket fences. Those with fire in their blood, those who hunger.

Originally published by the *Sudden Denouement Literary Collective*

Lady Justice

with Marcia J. Weber, Megha Sood, and Candice Louisa
Daquin

we keep justice
sealed under
bell-shaped glass
and morality
locked in amber
on our pristine
mantelpieces
we dust them off
from time to time
novelties to be
displayed
nonchalantly
when discerning guests
come to call
Christine E. Ray

                                        rest we now on our laurels?

weep, ye
lady liberty
/blind/
yet she sees
scales unbalanced
/hang/
justice
from the gallows
what say ye
from the gallery
/judge!/

181

when our pillars
are pilloried
/oh fair lady/
it's balls to the walls
in our halls
/to restore?/
of
justice
Marcia J. Weber

                              Languish in dubious lassitude?

times have changed now
who knows for better or worse,
Justice doesn't depend on the
severity now
depends on the numbers being judged;
a lone cry in the night
doesn't account for anything
unless it's compounded
with hashtags and March
Justice is not only blind
but deaf these days
piercing us;
like shards of glasses
left alone in the dark.
Megha Sood

                  or arise we thrusting sprouts of change?

scaling our hopes
dissected years float
weighing on bent necks
where lies the end of wrong?
step out from the curtain
shout your truth
change the world

erase lies, scrap the excuses
it's all or nothing
speak your mind
or lose it
there are no armchairs left
Candice Louisa Daquin

> *crash the gates of terror's reign?*
> *Marcia J. Weber*

Originally published on Heretics, Lovers, and Madmen

Curve Ahead
Elijah R. Carney

Feminist Manifesto

Feminism is my Realism
Kindra M. Austin

I am Organism
Female
Defense Mechanism
Natural
Feminism is my Realism
Because #MeToo, Motherfuckers
I've been abused
Been paid less cash
Called a Radical Cunt a
Bleeding Heart Liberal and
Put in my place—
Not my place, but theirs
I've been judged by the size of my body and clothes I wear
Been held back by (un)intelligent men and even stupider women
Who mock my Heart and Common Sense—
Slammed by Pseudo-Brain influenced by Meme Culture
I am Organism polluting the Cesspool
Feminism is my Realism
Kindra M. Austin

I am Organism
Female
Defense Mechanism
Instinctive
Feminism is my Realism
Because if I had been paid my 80 cents on the dollar
For every time I have been called
Bitch
Dyke

187

Ball breaker
Since I was 12 years old
I'd be in the damn 1%
Told my whole life
That I am
Too angry
Too emotional
Too loud
Too direct
Ask too many questions
Why-can't-you-just-sit-quietly-like-a-lady-and-smile-more?
Gagged with guilt to keep the peace
Gaslighted
so others can maintain the precious status quo
I am Virus circulating in the Bloodstream
Feminism is my Realism
Christine E. Ray

Originally published by *Whisper and the Roar. A Feminist Literary
Collective (& outlaw poets swearing)*

Sharp

with Kindra M. Austin, Megha Sood, Kristiana Reed,
Basiliké Pappa, Lois Linkens, Marcia J. Weber, Laurie
Wise, Iulia Halatz, and Sarah Doughty
A Weyward Sisters Collaboration

I am playing with knives
again
sharpening them
lovingly
against brown leather strap
admiring the way
hair splits cleanly
upon the well-honed edge
Christine E. Ray

Listen!
Sounds like a violin–
fine strings 'gainst steel bow
I play concerto
splitting hairs
Kindra M. Austin

I'm trimming those frayed ends
sharpening those
pointy convictions
giving them a sharp edge
a serrated opinion,
ready to pierce you
where it hurts you more
Megha Sood

Cold steel on skin,
I blossom,

stare down the line
take aim
at friend, foe and fortune
with my throwing knives;
multiply and divide,
split and survive.
Kristiana Reed

I like a razor
but xyraphi sings to me
of shreds, edges, ends
sweeter than silver cutlery.
An x is an eraser,
that's why I draw it long
to keep it clean and short
and save me complications.
Oh, how I love a razor!
Basiliké Pappa

There was a shadow crowd
And a circle of light. Sawdust stank
like dirty salt hair
And the thud
Against the board
Came like the footsteps of God.
Ribbons of air and time
Gathered round my ankles,
Coils of blue light.
Looping and curling and purring,
They crooned my power,
Sharp to draw blood from stone.
Lois Linkens

the slice was white lightening
lacerating flesh from bone
in the moment of searing truth.

I slash and gnash
my teeth barbed and keen
well-oiled from the feast
of my rotting soul.
I chop at the edges
of yesterday's sorrow
but the pain! I feel it not
only the blinding sting
of my wayward might
Marcia J. Weber

All the time in the world
Pressing down
Sharp as the obsidian
Black night
You relinquished me
To oblivion
Surviving on
Insidious pain
Of yesterday
Tapered to the edge
Of no tomorrow
Laurie Wise

I aim at dreams
knife them
as trophies on my wall.
I can always
take one down
quench the thirst
of a turbulent wound
with
tainted endearment
from the poisoned well
We dug and drained

191

under the wing of
One night.
I'm in love
with a stabbed dream.
Iulia Halatz

The blade cut into the night and flashed silver against the moonlight. And even though my ears heard no sounds but the thundering of my heart, I swore I could hear the sharp metal singing its high-pitched tune as it sliced through the air. It slipped through my skin like it was warm butter and at first I felt nothing. I wondered if maybe it was shock or disbelief. But then the pain started. Like someone injected gasoline into my bloodstream and lit a match. I watched as the thick, red liquid poured out of the fresh wound and begged for death. And as he stood over me, he licked my blood from his dagger and smiled down at me in a show of blood-stained teeth — right before everything went black.

When I awoke from the nightmare, I reminded myself that I was alive and the true face behind my fears liked it when I called him Daddy. The only comfort I found was knowing that death came for him first. Too bad he didn't take the memories with him.

Sarah Doughty

Originally published by the *Sudden Denouement Literary Collective*

Bird
Jharna Choudhury

Nevertheless, She Persisted

with Laurie Wise, Marcia J. Weber, Kindra M. Austin, and
Sarah Doughty
A Shield Maiden Collaboration

Her words, her will, her worth
Trampled and trodden
Forgotten
But for her
Flickering light
Fueled by ferocity
Molded with might
Courage compiled
Resilience reconciled
Wolves wryly grin
Circling again
Nevertheless, she persisted
Laurie Wise

She was told little girls
should be seen, not heard
but silence was suffocating
truth twisted in her stomach
razor sharp
when her voice finally rose
from a whisper
to a roar
they tried to drown her out
their indignation a cacophony
Nevertheless, she persisted
Christine E. Ray

194

Her initial protestations
propelled by burning bile
bubbling pique
in a voice squeaky
with disuse
were dubbed whining
she scrubbed corrosion
from rusted tongue
flexed, strengthening
articulate exclamation
strident
castrating
they proclaimed her
nevertheless, she persisted
Marcia J. Weber

Disregard your heart, they said
Faith is for the fools
Chasing gold; bold are the weak
Dream seekers
Dreams don't raise children
Nevertheless, she persisted
Kindra M. Austin

Silence was her solace,
the stillness of the night,
the calm before the storm.
Her voice, long since stifled.
Her body, long since defiled.
But they never broke her spirit.
Nevertheless, she persisted.
Sarah Doughty

Not Your Grandmother's Cross Stitch
Excerpt of 'No More' designed by Birdie's Crossing
Stitched by Christine E. Ray

Blurred Lines

line between art
and hate
chalked on the asphalt
has become blurred
smudged
by the feet that straddle it
insisting that all is fair
in creative expression
and war
do you get off sexually
on the violent images
you paint so graphically
of dismembered women's bodies
reduced to objects
things
for your craft?
or is it the thrill of attention you seek
from those who
break complicit silence
voice their outrage?
I sense an air of self-satisfied
intellectual superiority
from self-declared
provocateur
smugly letting the protests
roll off your back
confident in the belief
that we are unworthy wannabes
who cannot possibly appreciate your genius
your importance
as a true artiste

perhaps my resistance
to acknowledging your poetry (*literary snuff porn?*)
as high art
means I *am* a delicate little snowflake
I can live with that

What Do We Have Here?
Georgianna Grentzenberg

My Truth

my truth
my words
my blood
my bones
my tears
my pain
my joy
my heart
my soul
you may steal
my words
borrow
my sentences
appropriate
my verse
but my
fingerprints
have marked them
they are woven
like strands of my DNA
the essence of who I am
rings true
you will not
steal my voice
you shall not
steal my truth
forces far more powerful
far more fierce
than you
have tried to silence me
and still I stand

Carnivore

Jharna Choudhury

The Color of Our Rights
A Reproductive Rights Collaboration
with Jack Neece, Erin L. King, Megha Sood, Jamie Lynn
Martin, Candice Louisa Daquin, Susan M. Conway, Sarah
Doughty, Jesica Nordase, Saide Harb-Ranero, Quatrina
Hosain, Rachael Z. Ikins, and Robert Wertzler

I will wear red
for my sisters whose health is at risk
for my sisters who have been raped
for my sisters who have been battered
for my sisters who are already struggling
to feed hungry children
for my sisters who need to finish
middle school
high school
college
grad school
for my sisters who are just not prepared
I will wear crimson
for their lifeblood
that will spill in back alleys
that will stain
wire hangers
knitting needles
other unsterilized implements
that become their only choice
in a country that questions
their ability
their very right
to decide
Christine E. Ray

I have been seeing colors of all hues in my mind lately.
I walk down my street and notice the full bloom of the flowers.
Yellow daffodils.
Pink sunsets.
The rain brought growth and vitality.
Green grass.
My stomach turns as I am pulled from my spring daydream.
Clouds are forming. My colors change.
Red of the blood down her thighs
silver of the hanger of old
dark grey shadows
peeled white paint on a dirty van
purple bruises from unskilled hands—
how quickly we forget what our warrior women went through.
The fight has lost its color. Now all black and white. They can't
see in hues and block out truth.

I am a child in an orphanage. You scream my promise of a good home when I am unwanted. You tell me I will be saved by pro-life hands. I saw babies unwanted piled up like trash in a storage unit. Don't tell me about choice being wrong. I am a choice no one made. A ball dropped that no one caught. I am witness to what happens when no one cares. Stand behind your pulpit and up on your goddamn soap box and tell a soldier that was in the trench of state childcare what the options are. No one came for us. No one cuddled us on couches while they flipped through picture books with our faces in them. No one saved the smiles from the children as they slid off of their faces and hit the dirt. Many of my brothers and sisters in discard are dead now. Lost to a system you preach as an option. I watched the trash children we became. I brushed the hair of those lucky enough to be put up on the block as "New Mommy and New Daddy" walked the line. "Remember little one smile big and try to hide the sadness in your eyes. They will love you this time." We would stand like puppies in the window and pray for salvation. Our prayers would go unanswered. People shop for children like they shop for cars. I had my tires kicked a million times only to be left on the lot. I have the bruises to show for it. Unwanted throw away children become dangerous adults, or pretty young corpses.

Cover your eyes to the hues of color in this argument and the only colors we will see are those that run in the streets.

Jack Neece

Your body is obscene, cover it
uncover it and give it to me
or I'll cry "Frigid!" "Dyke!"
You are responsible for my anger.
Look at what you did!
If only you had listened.
Then I would hate you, slut, for giving me
what I want.
Erin L. King

False ownership—
this is strangely annoying—
when you see arrogance in
someone who doesn't own a thing.
Can't conjure a thing out of thin air
let alone a human being.
You are just the renter here. You don't own shit.
You are born from this womb
which cradles your existence for months
a sliver away from called a being.
Nothing but a pulsating existence in a foreign body.
Sometimes the body treats it like an infection
to keep away the contamination
self-purging, an act of reclamation.

Sometimes it accepts it
cups its own palm
supports you, carries it to term.
Its the body,
the arrangement
the unsaid understanding
a solemn promise
between the body and its identity.
Your existence is slowly molded
like a ball of sagging clay on the potter's wheel
morphed and molded
to be called a human being.
You don't own the womb.
You definitely don't own our bodies.
You break the arrangement—
just like to possess the things
Let me clear this up
for the sake of your understanding—
the body is not for your taking.
There is a thin line between
the choices we make and your wanting.
Megha Sood

She used to walk with a sparkle, gliding through the halls like the wind just blew her in. But what do you know about what it does to carry a reminder of the moment, of why your thighs scream at the sight of a man? To be ripped open, seed planted to bear his blighted fruit.

Her death was declared the moment you sold her womb to the devil. You man, with your flag drawn, throwing your words like they mean something. My body was not made to conquer!
Jamie Lynn Martin

Her mama told her / *your body is a temple girl* / *don't defile it or give it away* / she smoked and she drank to that / but when the boys mishandled her and something grew in her belly / she cried out loud / like a throttled nightingale / where is your justice? / the fires were lit / she anointed with shame / who better to be the brand bearer? / The rapists never knew her name / their child / their doing / sorry you can't use that as an excuse / there are no relief for women who are abused / you should want to cradle your rapists child / here, give me the umbilical chord / let it sound in the dark / no succor here for survivors of incest and rape / lest men not control the uterus / oh lord heaven forbid / she burns with shame / they chant in unison / blood blood / we own your ovaries and private parts / the rape is divided / once and then again / when the law did not defend her / such is the pyre of women / born to defend their shame / inherited over generations / will it ever stop?

Candice Louisa Daquin

My knee jerk reaction is to start swinging blindly, hoping to connect with something old, red-faced, white, and male. As I raise my opened claws, exposing the softest flesh of my pink outstretched palms, I realize that this plays directly into the hands of the predator. I am not a predator, but I have spent my whole life sensing the shadows that pass o'er, discerning their threat levels, dodging them, knowing how they hunt, and how they think.

I am Mouse, master of disguises; now you see me, now you don't.

I remember who I am and retreat to the safety of the thicket, just as the shadow swoops down, knowing they got me where they want me, and now they're gonna eat me. I do not accept that I am on the menu today, Mr. Eagle; nor will I any other day. I will claw my way from your throat beast. Know that I will bite back until the beat has abandoned my chest and my body is made of sunshine and moonlight.

When Source asked would you rather be a Top Predator or Smart Prey, you chose your lot Mr. Eagle. You failed to remember that sustainability is not found in rumbling through jungles roaring fear me and eating everything in sight. You will be left starving. Left to rot, your ribcage will become our homes until they turn to fertile soil that makes way for generations to gather, feasting on your fallen kind's sweetmeats. We be small, but we be mighty.
Susan M. Conway

It was the white-hot sun, glaring down at me, pressing its warmth against the fresh, purple bruises I'd hidden beneath my clothes. It was the silvery-blue moonlight and occasional yellowed headlights that lit my room at night while I laid awake and waiting. It was the way his voice slid like black ice down my spine, the scent of cigarettes and beer on his breath, making the blood moving through my veins turn cold, freezing me from the inside out. That was the fear. That was the hatred. That was what awaited me. Every day, and every night. Where was justice then?

What about the countless other young girls experiencing the same fate? What of the ones forced to carry the children of their abusers? The ones that now have a government choosing for them how they use their bodies? What of the ones with no money, no assistance, and no means to survive on their own — newborn infant in their weary arms with crimson blood dripping down their legs? Where was the help when they starved or froze to death on the streets? What can we do when we have no rights over our own bodies no matter where we go?

Sarah Doughty

My heart is a rainbow of colors.
Loves with no restraint.
"Tame that sinful heart" they say, because it loves both women and men.
"Your body is a temple" they say.
But what they really mean, is that it's a church, whitewashed and filled with stories of how women began pain.
My innocence was never hues of pastel, it was a currency to be exchanged for a worthy husband, who'd tame what my father couldn't ... so I gave it away.
The red of my blood as it stained my school pants, was tangible proof that I now was another sinful woman that had to learn her place.
The green of the grass I laid my head upon, left imprints on my summer clothes and instead of wondering what fields I graced with my dreams, you demanded to know why I laid in public with such lack of propriety.
When my body bloomed suddenly, my clothes all became sins, and the hate from school teachers spewed over my young physique ... making stains of dark spit and vile on my white uniform.
The shadows now darken so many neon souls, who simply want control of the vessel they inhabit, who refuse to bow to archaic laws.
The inky black of evil, threatens to infect the world we are building for our future daughters and sons.
They spew their hate and condemn what they will never understand.
But the sun will shine again.
We will fight for it
tooth and nail.
You've taken enough.
Your power will run its course.

We refuse to go on living in the shadows of your consent.
Let your flag fly.
Let freedom ring.
Jesica Nordase

Raised in a green, faraway land where
women lack power over our bodies,
all while stepping on fertile soils,
left to be watered by the hand of an oppressor.
No voiced cries, no souls to heal anymore;
just vacant shells left behind to pick up the pieces of what was
once called a woman.
No resistance to stop the invasion either —
just compliance to carry appointed commands.
A woman should always know her place in the world, His world.
A Man's world.
Makes it easier to endure.
Problem solved, right? So I thought.
As a teen, I witnessed so many injustices:
sex, unprotected by foolish teenagers.
Rape, hushed just so a community never faced shame brought
in without consent.
Victims blamed, the easiest outcome to digest.
The solution, girls forced to marry their rapist, only to restore
honor to the family...
Problem solved, right? So I was told.
Eight dollars and fifty cents, the American dollar equivalent of a
problem solved.
A pill handed to girls by desperate mothers in the family
bathroom.
No doctor. No care. No precautions.
"Just go to sleep. It will go away overnight."
That overnight hell comes and goes, leaving scars, with no elixir

to kill the pain of a physical and emotional trauma
of waking up in a puddle of her own crimson blood.
But that's okay. It's never talked about again. It's over.
Problem solved, right? So I heard.
But now I'm here.
A red, white, and blue flag held high above my head, giving me a
sense of protection.
Of 'I am home.'
A humongous sign, "The land of the free," brought tears to my
eyes while walking through Customs.
"Welcome to the United States of America, Miss,"
he told me as he handed me the passport that carried so much
pain I wanted to forget.
I was free. I am free.
My body is safe now.
I am my own woman.
Problem solved, right? So I hoped.
But where the hell am I?
Am I in a country where rights are protected,
where voices are heard,
Where strength and free will is celebrated?
Or am I in a third-world country again?
I woke up confused that morning.
With two girls I needed to get ready for school.
Two girls I had been lying to, apparently.
Telling them they have rights.
That they're strong.
That they are lucky they were born here and not overseas.
Problem solved, right? Or so I thought.
I woke up confused that morning.
Reading a law that condemns a rape victim to carry her abuser's
child.
Forcing women to resort to unsafe solutions, any means in order

to take away a pain that they didn't deserve.

I woke up confused that morning.

Wondering, why was a law, regarding a woman's body, made by misogynistic Men?

Someone, please, wake me from this nightmare, calm my heart, and assure me that this is not a world my daughters are being raised in.

What's the solution? I wonder.

Saide Harb-Ranero

My body will not be affected
By decisions of men in legislatures
I do not spill crimson every month.
My body will not be affected
By men carrying knives and ligatures
I cannot be raped.
My body will not be affected
By men who decide women need not study
I already have a college degree.
My body will not be affected
By men who declare I can't work
My husband pays all the bills.
So they relaxed their bodies
In willful blindness.
They laughed at sisters
Who marched on the streets.
They joined the men in calling them whores.
And said their sons were worth more.
Then came laws that forced darkness
Faces forced behind cloaks of bleakness.
The marchers were murdered
The voices silenced.
Dance outlawed, music banned.
Writers fled, poets quietened.

Memories of the Taliban
Became realities again.
In lands that had assumed
Never again.
Quatrina Hosain

More than Wage Inequality- Nightly News- a May week in 2019
"Missouri restricts abortion rights! Alabama has already made it
illegal."
"I choose life!"
No, you choose a ball of cells with no heartbeat-technically as
alive as an amoeba, over a woman.
"A 19 yr old pregnant woman was murdered by 2, a mother and
daughter. They opened her belly, cut out her unborn baby to
raise as their own."
Was she a container the prize was in to toss into a dumpster?
"US pregnancy rates are down! so low we can't replace the
population! The reason: most significant, the drop in teen
pregnancy."
Fewer humans would allow some of the one million species in
the verge of extinction because of human depredation of the
planet
a chance to
choose life.
In the midwest, fine American women hired an Ivy League-
educated woman physician to remove the entire genitalia from a
6 yr old girl.
No anesthetic, grandmother, mother held the little girl down.
Sewn-shut breeding machines
in the name of one version of God.
Lawyers and legislators debate whether to call it "child abuse" or
"freedom of religion"
to justify doing nothing.

Historically women underwent hysterectomies for everything
from depression to
back pain to
a hang nail.
I ask you.
If a man complains of headaches, will you cut off his balls?
We march.
We are loud.
Yet the juggernaut blunders forward.
Back to a place where it's encouraged to grab pussy because
"they love it!"
Let me grab you by the balls.
"Le plus ça change, le plus que c'est la même chose."
I am a woman of an age where society deems me invisible and
irrelevant. My gray hairs, my wrinkled skin.
A woman friend messaged me recently, "at our age the light
begins to dim." Sure, talk yourself into it.
My light BLAZES because
I OWN MY LIFE.
I am just getting started so
BACK THE FUCK OFF!
Rachael Z. Ikins

I don't know what color to wear
For the child of rape forced to accept
Her mother's rapist as Father
For that mother forced to put her daughter
Into the hands of her rapist
For the grieving mother mourning a miscarried child
And under investigation for possible homicide
For the child of incest
Life-long symbol of a family's shame
For the doctor who must make a judgment call
On a woman's life or a doomed fetus and

212

Facing 99 years if a court disagrees
No, I don't know the right color to wear
Black of grief?
Rage red?
What color is fear?
Perhaps Gold for resolve that
These horrors must not come to pass
Robert Wertzler

Originally published by *Heretics, Lovers, and Madmen*

I Dissent
Excerpt from 'Little Sarcy Witch' designed by Sarcy Girl
Stitched by Christine E. Ray

What say you, America?!
June 26, 2022

As I continue to mull over the events of the last week, several thoughts have crossed my mind.

Given the Supreme Court's ruling on gun rights, I think ALL women in the United States should consider purchasing a gun to help assist them in preventing unplanned pregnancies. In fact, arming women and girls could become a popular public health campaign.

"Wear two condoms. Or else."

In fact, generously arming all women and girls could be effective in reducing the incidence of rape and sexual assaults. If 'one good guy with a gun' can prevent a mass shooting, imagine what an entire society of furious armed women and girls could do?!

I think it's time for men to take the lead in preventing unplanned pregnancies. They are the more 'mature' and 'rational' sex, right?!

I recommend that any man or boy who would like to have sex with someone with a uterus should be required to carry a federally issued ID card indicating whether they are fertile, have had a vasectomy, or are otherwise naturally infertile. In fact, I think providing vasectomies could become an emerging industry in the United States.

Perhaps a portion of the profits earned on the sales of Viagra™ and Cialis™ and other treatments for erectile dysfunction could be channeled into new federally subsidized drive-up vasectomy clinics.

And finally, instead of repealing Lawrence v. Texas and/or Obergefell v. Hodges, I instead recommend generous tax breaks for those who choose same-sex marriage. It's simply good economics.

Think of all the taxpayer money that could be saved in the long run by reducing the cost incurred prosecuting and incarcerating women and girls with the audacity to think they should control their own reproduction?!

What say you, America?!

Forged of Flame

with Kindra M. Austin, Marcia J. Weber, Laurie Wise and
Sarah Doughty
A Shield Maiden Battle Song

The fire that whelms me does
not consume; for it is mine
own—
I do control inferno,
a blood-borne lust to conquer
pain—
Here you come with buckets of water,
and a head distended with ego
convinced I'm a woman in distress
The fire that whelms me does
not consume; for it is mine
own—
my defense mechanism,
desire to live forged in
flame—
Shield Maiden calls for no goddamned man
Kindra M. Austin

these flames that fence me
char me not
they are the hungering tongues
of my animus
I spark them
cerise
feeding them on
the oxygen of my outrage
when the world crushes
upon me

you hasten forward
all suited up
toting your much touted hose
as if your stream
could touch these flames
these flames that fence me
char me not
they are the hungering tongues
of my animus
I fan them
as Hestia and her sisters
lit by my righteous fury
under deluge of
hypocrisy incomprehensible
your rushing consternation holds no candle to my Warrior
woman flames
Marcia J. Weber

this blaze that engulfs me
comes not from without
but within
it is the passion
the rage
that simmers deep in my core
hot roiling lava
that has churned
in the souls of warrior women
for thousands of years
we are fire
we are stone
you fancy yourself a mage
brandishing flashes of lightening
ominous clouds
with a studied flick of your wrist

believing that your cold, soaking rain
can extinguish what burns within me
I laugh as your efforts
evaporate into mist
chest deflated
your hubris
sags to your knees
Christine E. Ray

Enveloped in an inferno
yet scorched, I am not
For this is my torch
of triumph
An act of defiance
Warrior woman alliance
summoning strength
You, with your shining armor,
prowl around pleading pluvial persuasions,
beware, lest I steal your air, fueling the flames,
and smother you in a fiery back-draft.
Enveloped in an inferno
yet scorched, I am not
It is my self-sparked
simmering sustenance
dissuading demons
Always ablaze
Lighting the way
Anemic armor melts from the heat of Warrior Women united in
courageous combustion
Laurie Wise

I felt this power rushing through my veins like a drug, searing
every cell as it passed and transformed the very marrow in my
bones to obsidian. My skin grew thicker, no longer the flawless

flesh it once was, but marred by memories and shielded from what was to come. My eyes no longer reflected the sea, but instead burned like the sun.

No longer was I the innocent child, but the woman, risen from her own ashes. Ready to battle the very demons that haunted me, broken me, and left me to rot.

I became flame. I became fury.

I became my own savior.

Sarah Doughty

Testify!

with Nicholas Gagnier, Stephen Fuller, Megha Sood,
Sarah Doughty, Candice Louisa Daquin, Kindra M. Austin,
Marcia J. Weber, and Susan M. Conway

Elephants in the arena,
drowning out the stories as
we all hear them,
stomping on
the flowerbed scenery
they've built around your garden of rot,
and without a
second thought,
sold the world a
wilting centerpiece
Nicholas Gagnier

I
And his daughter prayed for her
She didn't really know why
She prayed she'd not meet a guy
At a party; 'cause he'd liked beer
That sudsy stuff she'd now fear
II
The louder we toast
The better the truth we spew
Just another pint
The truth becomes toxic stew
We'll all agree
Got the votes of the old crew
Now let's all meet
At Four P's and grab a brew
Stephen Fuller

Oh! Look at him
when the venom drips from his slithering tongue
and he moans and screams
to validate his flagrant lies
and the white privilege
agrees in complete unison
Hiding behind the female prosecutor
those bunch of naysayers,
shreds and rips reality into bits and pieces
she should have reported it sooner
where the validity of her truth never mattered
it would never be
a grain of sand in their eyes of ignorance
too hard to ignore,
too painful to realize
an exercise in futility.
Megha Sood

If only I knew
that high school and college
were hunting grounds
for people like you.
The ones that worked hard
with all their money,
physical talent, and popularity.
Those predators were untouchable.
Little did I know that being
in an empty hallway,
a bus ride at night,
or walking home from school
was a dangerous act.
If only I knew that predators
come in all forms,
and not all monsters

have hideous faces.
The word of a quiet, unknown girl
would never match
the thoroughbred males
that dominated my world.
If speaking up would only lead
to more labels, accusations, and bullying,
why say anything at all?
The shame and guilt
was already overwhelming.
Why add insult to injury — literally?
Sarah Doughty

Get out of my head
my body, my bed
take your license for molesting
somewhere they welcome it
there's no show tonight
the actress fled the stage
finding herself unable to fake
why bruises keep cropping up
like blooms of rot on her body
the price paid for her art
they told everyone she wanted
to be gang-banged at the after party
where lilies to congratulate her success
lay strewn on much trod floors
as they ground her soul to flour
she felt the wink out of valor
how can I go on from this?
Where is my sword? My strength
to rise above their dissection and
penchant for ownership with violate
lend me a knife so I can slice

their pretty little grins of entitlement
right off their wolfish mouths
Candice Louisa Daquin

Liar!
the self-righteous hiss
under their breath and
in the comments sections
their venom dripping deep
so like their ancestors
who spit *Witch!* and
Whore
from forked tongues
when truth spoken
shattered the community
myths
Christine E. Ray

Devil's dancing fingers go
clickety-clack,
tapping at the keys,
and shifty voices surge.
Virulence is vomited into microphones:
"She lies!"
Meanwhile, we continue
to learn that some of our friends are despicable people—
discover stomach turning rhetoric and defense of abusers.
Women blaming women…
I'm fuckin disgusted by all the questions:
"Why didn't you report this sooner?"
"Why did you put yourself in that situation, anyway?"
"Why even bother speaking out now?"
We're under attack,
and I'm armed to the nines.
Kindra M. Austin

you formed thick callouses
padding o'er those wounds
I watched how you bled
as you peeled them off.
you held your composure
just so
/a shield and your frying pan/
at arms' length
peering from behind spectacles
uttering carefully poured
analytical professorial articulations.
I saw you shake
we all did
your sisters in conversant
solidarity.
I bled alongside you
as you clawed off your skin
in the service of truth
that bitch named
greater good
and I felt the warm sanguinary
drip
as your demons feasted
on your vulnerable flanks
all the while.
he is laughing still
isn't he?
Marcia J. Weber

The abuse began so long ago that I can't quite place a finger on the exact moment my heart shattered for the first time. I don't have an "I remember it so vividly" story, for that moment, because there is so much water – so much water between me and the shore. I want so badly to plant my anchors of feet into that wet sand and refuse to budge ever again. But my reality is one of drowning and resuscitation; only to end up with another mouthful of water and flailing hands. Memories do fade, especially when the waves do not relent. But, it doesn't make the assault or the sting nonexistent. Must we bleed all over you in order for you to believe? By the power of 3 × 3 karma let them see. Let them see. As I will it, so mote it be.

Susan M. Conway

Originally published on *Blood Into Ink: Warrior Voices of Survival*

Songs of Ophelia

with Rana Kelly, Lois Linkens, Sun Hesper Jansen,
Basiliké Pappa, Iulia Halatz, Allister Nelson, and Candice
Louisa Daquin
A Weyward Sisters Collaboration

You must remember
Rosemary, pansies, fennel,
Columbine and rue,
You forgot tansy, didn't you?
When the ground freezes over
And your flowers crumble and brown
Let the ice in hamlet's heart
And the red on his hands
Deliver him forever from you.
And when you return again
From your journey to the sea
Never forget
It is you.
It was never he.
Rana Kelly

from up here, the night is clearer.
she is closer to the sky.
branches cradle like a mother's arm,
bouncing in the night's distractions.
if she stretches high enough,
perhaps the summer breeze
will whip these leaves into a flurry,
and carry her to meet the star-girls
she longs,
yet a maternal clasp

226

holds her fast,
with ropes of hot blood.
Lois Linkens

My orisons remember
ever more sins than yours.
This cage of my ribs—
infested with specters
that would have broken you
long ago—opens to a world
beyond flowers, beyond air.
I breathe out the curse of you.
I breathe in the maternal deep.
I am already becoming
a heartbeat underwater,
a wild pulse restored at last
to a rhythm long denied.
I am dancing my way,
slowly, to the sea.
Sun Hesper Jansen

My purpose is to serve,
father,
king,
lover.
So let me serve.

Here is your wine — honeyed and spiced, like your words to me, father; remember? Spoken, no doubt, from love and care. "You are my daughter," you said, "you will do as I say." Drink now, father, a gift of obedience and devotion in this cup, brewed with my hand. And as you drink, let me tell you of my walks along the river. Not a single violet grows on its banks; just many a white flower. Drink, dear father, and let me feel my power.

My king, here is your cup, filled to the brim. Drink; mind not the bite behind the sweet. And as I tell you of a willow that weeps no more, pay no heed to the stories of a girl. Think only of the kiss of

227

gold against your lips; of other ways I can serve your schemes —
ah, yes, the kingdom. Drink, my king, and let me find my freedom.

This is a wine fit for philosophers — and you, sweet prince. What
did you ever give me besides talk, talk, talk? Drink, and when you
drain your cup, pray talk some more — say, can you taste me on
your tongue? Wild hemlock and nightshade: such are the flowers
of my heart. No roses left — they withered you know when. Or
perhaps you don't, busy as you are crying over the dead. Drink,
my love. Your self-indulgent aches, your oh-so-profound thoughts
this wine will ease. Drink, sweet prince, and leave me in peace.

For you, no more Ophelia,
father,
king,
lover.
I am my own Ophelia.
Basiliké Pappa

defined always
by men around me
daughter
sister
virgin
whore
locked ever in memory
who holds the keys
to my prison?
descent into
watery madness
sink gracefully
into welcoming embrace
i will become a mermaid
a siren
no room on dry land

228

in this man's world
for a woman of pure heart
to break the mold
break expectation
my fight floats away...
Christine E. Ray

I long for a dream,
within a dream
that clears the sight
of you.
I am asleep and asleep
I feel nothing
But the cradle of your arms
like orange snakes
thrashing fears around...
Black and white tale
Shall that be...
Every night a little dream
in the dead of sleep
in the depth of you...

Words spatter lights
in pools.
Do not squander their yellow glare
To guard you through winter...
Iulia Halatz

the water is deep, Ophelia
pennants of your hair, ghost-like
in the autumnal freeze. your body
is a ship to steer through the lilies,
and to Hell's gate you row, your
strong bones now eaten by frogs.

Hamlet rots, but you proved true,
woman lives on, man dies, is dust.

pale among the reeds, silence.
"i gave my kingdom for freedom,"
she whispers, and in salvation,
knows.
Allister Nelson

Do you see me winking
Beneath the violet hour in
Perpetual rest, I slumber, mouth
Agape the hour of my quiet, soft is
Silence underwater, where flowers
Turn their drowsy heads into dream
I see only, visions of myself in silver
Where once I galloped wild and feral
In a world unused to strong headed girls
They wanted me submerged under glass
To keep my knowledge in little jars
I stuffed them so full they shattered
And now I am still, in facsimile, watching out
The world of aches still turning slow
I lent my breath to the wild moors
For they will listen, they will know
Candice Louisa Daquin

Moody Flower
Elijah R. Carney

Back to Black: Tribute to Amy Winehouse

with Rana Kelly, Lois Linkens, Aakriti Kuntal, Marcia J.
Weber, Kindra M. Austin, Rachel Finch, Sarah Doughty,
Laurie Wise, and Zelda Raville
A Weyward Sisters

Oh, Amy
Whenever I go walking
In my stilettos,
I hear you talking.
Dream me up a way
Of swishing my hips
And pursing my lips
And singing your riffs
So that I find beauty
Like you.
Rana Kelly

she puts on her black dress in the dark,
anxious red nails messy
in bleary, sleeping artistry.
he left the candle burning
in the winter window –
vanilla and cinnamon and cool
on a Sunday evening,
tears on a Monday.
last week's relief
breathes
into tonight's regrets,
but the shadowy smear
on the glass
is all that is left of him.
Lois Linkens

Rummaging through
black air,
nauseous red nails bearing oily seas
Suffocating
existence with conversations,
conversations
with glittering nail cutters,
cracked moons
laughing hysterically in them
Conversations
of fallen boyfriends, of fallen love
Fallen being
the new being
Aakriti Kuntal

She scrawls lines
up the back of her fishnet stockings
wiggly-lined intoxicated rebellion
strutting down memory lane
flirting shamelessly with self-destruction
as if, in seductive self-abasement
she may reclaim
love from a wayward lover
and from self
Marcia J. Weber

Kohl black kitty cat
Eyes
Lines stiletto sharp
Tongue dipped in honey
Wine(house), oh, Amy
Slay me
Kindra M. Austin

Night chimes, a ringing to remind her,
She can sleep the day away, but the dark
still draws the Soul from the body.
Stars reflecting off bottles, empty, their
contents alive in her throat.
She is midnight, waking the world.
Rachel Finch

I remember how you carried your beauty like body armor, letting the world see a smoke screen that many didn't notice. I remember seeing the sadness beneath those wings on your eyes, the way your mouth curled into a devilish smile. I remember seeing your hair down, with those curls that lasted for miles, and how much I wanted just a tiny piece of your beauty. Your essence. Even a little piece of your ability to hold the world in bated breath. I remember your courage to stand in front of a million people and hold them under your spell. But what I remember the most is how you wore your heart on the outside and how pieces of it were broken away and lost over time, exposing you. Like a nerve within a broken tooth, you tried to insulate, but nothing could fix what you'd already lost.
Sarah Doughty

Hiding in plain sight
Black songbird
Aching to be heard
Darker than the darkest shadows
Praying sacrificial hymns
Will carry away your demons
Hungry hearts rapture in melody
Enchanted with your euphony
An intentional symphony
Desperate on bended knee
Longing to be set free

Blood and wine
Cherry lipstick stains
Broken bottles
Crooked lines
Sing for us
One last time
Laurie Wise

Our biggest tragedy
was that
our love,
no matter
how much
there was of it
could never
draw you out
from a fatal attraction
to the depths
of your ferocious hunger
for love itself.
Zelda Raville

you shot across our heavens
a piercing silver whiskey light
your pain-soaked voice
etching a pin-up girl tattoo on our souls
We died a hundred times with you
Donning our mourning colors
we are left to only say goodbye with words
as your heartbreaking beauty
fades into black
Christine E. Ray

Originally published by the *Sudden Denouement Literary Collective*

Velvet Glove

Marcia J. Weber

The Burning Bed

with Marcia J. Weber, Laurie Wise, Dom Wynette, and
Kindra M. Austin
A Shield Maiden Collaboration

memories float about like smoke from a raging wildfire
unsure if I should run or hide
a conflicting desire to hold on and release
breathe in, breathe out
shaking, quaking
I need them to stay
I need them to go
Marcia J. Weber

> chafing of my bondage
> sparked a rope burn
> it smoldered inside me
> tonguing greedily upon my soul
> it fed on the fuel of my fears
> igniting red-orange on my flesh
> licking with scarlet-steel flames
> through the cracked parchment
> shell of my skin
> *Laurie Wise*

I think I am supposed to hate this encounter… possibly hate it
and me enough to love it.
I don't know if I need it to stop… or if I just need to see where it
will go… the pain is so parallel to my pleasure…
Yet all that I feel is the heat from this burning bed… it's hot like
fire as my arsonist whispers in my ear… his words… *"you like
it…"* are swirling around my head…

More like bouncing like a sick game of ping pong... or possibly a
dirtier game... something so wrong...
Or is it right?
The fire in my loins can't be extinguished... my body betrays me
over and over and she doesn't fight...
Dom Wynette

it started as fire
the slow red flame that licked up my walls
before you showed me Jekyll and Hyde
as you knock me to the floor
for what I decide
will be the last damn time
I realize I have turned to a woman of ice
blood from my split lip frozen to my chin
frost on my skin that will burn
your fingers if you lay your hands on me again
Christine E. Ray

Label me crazy with ink black, blue, and red;
You beat up my body,
Raped away my identity,
Fucked up my head.
Is my insanity so temporary?
I wonder while you burn.
Kindra M. Austin

Originally Published by *Blood Into Ink: Warrior Voices of Survival*

Thread 2
Jharna Choudhury

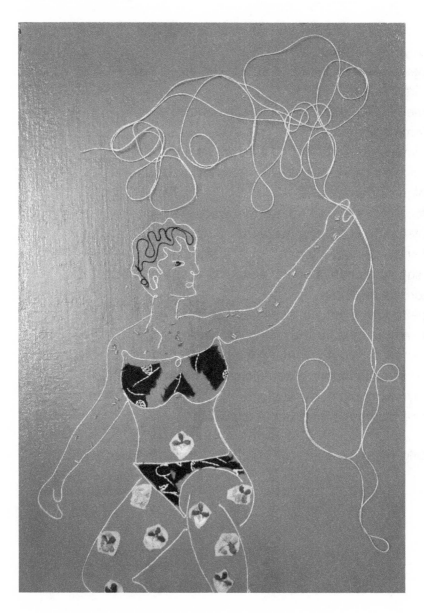

I Knew My Worth
Kindra M. Austin

I knew my worth when I was hot as fuck and
boys all lined up to
pet my cleft at the blind side of the playground—
dirty fingers
mercifully uneducated in the intricacies of
female anatomy
I knew my worth when I was hot as fuck in
middle school, despite my flat chest and
highly guarded cleft—
face of Helen and an ass that wouldn't quit,
by the gods, I knew my worth
I knew my worth when I was hot as fuck and
high school boys poorly educated in the delicacies of
female anatomy
petted my cleft with excavating fingers—
I sang hymns for my molested hymen
I knew my worth when I gave birth
two weeks before graduation, and I was in love;
my sweet babe, my savior—
she taught me the truth of my worth

Originally published by *Blood Into Ink: Warrior Voices of Survival*

I Knew My Pain

Marcia J. Weber

I knew my pain when it was a screeching
sunset
spurting cotton candy carnage
across the feathered heavens
mocking all that is soft and soothing
drawing my gaze
up and up, tearstained
\thundering scarlet refrains\
reverberating clang of your loss.
I knew my pain when it was a snarling
saber-tooth
birthed of my rent ventricles
spewing aortic dirges
feasting on festering anguish
\clamorous gluttony\
heartache grew fangs
fueled on midnight howling
and my heart gnawed raw itself.
I knew my pain when it was a stinging
nettle
clinging needy-puppy to my shins
\all scratch and scrape reminders\
of the bite that replaced the soul
in the deep chocolate of your iris.
I knew my pain when it was creeping
ivy
camouflaged among wistful greening
arisen from the fetid heap
\itching a glitch in my hopeful healing\

tendrils sneak snake-oil slick
renders my skin hopeless raw
where it lingered
in the shadow of your touch.
I knew my pain when it was tempered
steel
inlaid with soulful etchings
\mother of my surviving pearl soul\
I raise the blades coated
in my fevered blood
hammered now, the plowshares
of my hard-won stance.

Originally published by *Whisper and the Roar. A Feminist Literary Collective (& outlaw poets swearing)*

I knew My Invisibility

Candice Louisa Daquin

I knew my invisibility when
the lady next to my mother in the nursing ward
took me in her arms out of pity
for there was nobody there who cared
to rock a crying child, who was not wanted
by hedonists who erred in pregnancy
I knew my invisibility when
my mother tucked bus ticket in her blouse
kissed me goodnight for the final time
explaining she needed to get out and breathe
did not remember to keep the door ajar
and the night vanquished me in her absence
I knew my invisibility when
my father silently resented single-parenting
did not pick me up outside the school gates
the boys in the projects threw stones and jeered
shouted "show me your stinking snatch, bitch"
until I learned to climb trees and wait and wait and wait
I knew my invisibility when
my grandfather told me to sit on his lap
the only attention was the wrong kind and sick
everyone else got busy like they didn't know what was
happening
bit like being chained to a rock and watching for The Gorgon
I knew my invisibility when
my friends in bikinis had boys stuck to them like bees
cooing as birds will underneath willow trees
whilst I was bitten by mosquitos not men

and the ordinariness of me was the best repellent
no need to spray tan, just stand and burn
I knew my visibility when
I broke into pieces and watched them descend
unwilling to drown I reached out and a hand pulled
me out of the darkness and into her universe
where for the first time I was seen and loved
for who I was and not a cream centered assortment
Blindly plucked from a candy box

Originally published by Whisper and the Roar: A Feminist Literary
Collective (& outlaw poets swearing): *A Feminist Literary Collective (&
outlaw poets swearing)*

I Know My Worth
Devereaux Frazier

I know my worth
Are you sure about that?
They ask me in the twilight hours
Caressing the vain sense and sensibilities
Of someone already caught in the eye
Storms vast, lighting strikes wide and deadly
The waves toss my hapless soul overboard
And plunge me deep into the abyss of sorrows
But alas, they are not my own
Not mine to keep
Just bitter tales of man and woman
Too deep in love to remain apart
When the fates have aligned they should
Swords run through aghast faces
Spears pluck the youth from their mothers
And leave carcasses piled high to heaven
Are you sure you know your worth?
When everyone around you is bleeding
And everything is choking on the blood
Not of their own, and not of yours
But of their forefathers, and all their mistakes
How blessed can life truly be when pain
Is served for each and every meal
There is no remedy for the man of burden
Toiling away, he writes his passions in the dust
With each breath he loses a day
But gains a star in the ever present firmament
One day I too will join my star family
One day I will know what it means to be home

So when they ask me
Are you sure you know your worth?
I will say no
Because as long as I'm here I cannot say
My path has hardly started, and goals
Simply fooled with
But those who come after me can say
Without an inkling of doubt
Who I was
Yes, we knew his worth
In the world he created, we too can create
And in continuing on the path of peace
Redeem the time so solemnly granted
And eagerly withdrawn

Originally published by *Whisper and the Roar: A Feminist Literary Collective (& outlaw poets swearing)*

There Were Things I Did Not Know
Lois Linkens

There were things I did not know (could not know).
There were words I was yet to write, a still
Small voice, yet to claim. 'Tis life's greatest thrill,
To light an unknown match, and watch it glow.
I would do great things. I would swing my feet
O'er fences, walls, tall gates to walk amid
The places I had never seen, and bid
Farewell to my young self, to future meet.
Places that could hold me fast, scoop me out
And fill me with their beads, their jasmine ways.
Here comes tomorrow in its dusky haze.
I have seen the future, soon green to sprout.
Where so much is known today, I decree
To hold the great surprise, and startle me.

Originally published by *Whisper and the Roar. A Feminist Literary
Collective (& outlaw poets swearing)*

I Knew My Faults

Sarah Doughty

"I knew my faults.
And they always stared
back at me in the mirror."
As long as I can remember, I knew my faults. They were engraved in my flesh, repeated so often that even I saw nothing else. I knew every one. Believed every one. I was every one.
I knew my faults when I was toddling around, learning how to speak, how to walk, how to cower.
I knew my faults when I began school. How I wasn't smart enough, not social enough. How I was a target in school. And at night.
I knew my faults in the dark. I learned my best to do what was required of me, but I was never quite good enough. I knew what my hands needed to do, how my lips should stay soft, or how my hips were supposed to move with the right timing. After awhile, I knew those moves just enough to get by.
I knew my faults. And they always stared back at me in the mirror.

Originally published by *Whisper and the Roar. A Feminist Literary Collective (& outlaw poets swearing)*

I Knew My Purpose
Rachel Finch

I knew my purpose
when little legs were
thrust apart,
foreign hands molding my body
into a better fit for themselves,
shaping my form and my future.
I knew my purpose when they
took their turns and the skin on
my face didn't burn beneath the salt,
but soaked it into every pore with a
remembering.
I knew my purpose when the
bruises painted my inner thighs
and even my silent lips couldn't
hide the gospel.
I knew my purpose when the tears fell and
only the birds were listening.
Shades of hurt patterned my flesh and I was
already living in the knowing.
I would grow wings and beat them to the
sound of every whimper of a sister
and I would turn the betrayal into a war cry
for peace and justice

Originally published by *Whisper and the Roar. A Feminist Literary Collective (& outlaw poets swearing)*

I Knew My Fate
Laurie Wise

I knew my fate when
Enraged voices penetrate
Vulnerable
Eyes closed tight
Dreaming of locks
Picked and set free
I knew my fate when
Words embedded
Forever me
Followed by scenes
Violent
Seen and unseen
I knew my fate when
Heart carried weight
Haunted
Day and night
Searching for savior
Bury the burden
I knew my fate when
Reflection revealed
Strength intrinsic
Click
An open door
Running no more

Originally published by *Whisper and the Roar: A Feminist Literary Collective (& outlaw poets swearing)*

I Knew My Stature
Marcia J. Weber

I knew my stature when I was a shrinking violet
wilting wallflower
hangdog hanging in the corner of the gym
stewing in the stench of pubescent sweat
and hurricanic hormonal surges
a bit too fleet of mind
and broad of hip
to be asked to dance.
I knew my stature when I was a shriveling teen
angularly angling
for acceptance in the seat of those size 4 jeans
gaunt of cheek and lean on ease
I nibbled on the knowledge
skinny girls get dated
while I wasted \wishing\ away.
I knew my stature when I was a curvaceous coed
unholstering my sexuality
like the black market weapon it was
filed down and ripe for the bidding
overpowered and unequipped for battle
shooting myself in the foot
greenhorn that I was.
I knew my stature when I was a birthing Bessie
nursing \wet and dry\
bequeather of sustenance and succor
repository of binkies, hugs and tissues
beneath notice as an independent woman
selling my soul for a closed bathroom door.
I knew my stature when I strode that shore

clove in rhythm
with the seething tides
shedding the skin
of a thousand judging serpents
one with the wilding waves
as they sing my siren song.

Originally published by *Whisper and the Roar: A Feminist Literary Collective (& outlaw poets swearing)*

I Knew My Lesson
Megha Sood

I knew my lesson
when your touch left the scar
again and again on
my suppurating skin
and you remain unscathed
and free
I knew my lesson
when crying under the
covers and
keeping those lips pursed
made no difference to your
ignorant smirk and
your bouts of glee
I knew my lesson
when I tried to please you
and kept crushing my own
desires
losing the tourniquet to
set myself-free
I knew my lesson
when I had to choose between
the dream
and the rancid choices
you gallantly offered me
I knew my lesson

when in the relationship
I ended my self
trying to ignite the love in "we"

Originally published *by Whisper and the Roar: A Feminist Literary Collective (& outlaw poets swearing)*

Submerged Leaves

Elijah R. Carney

I Knew My Heart
Eric Syrdal

I knew my heart
when boys were boys
and making her cry meant you liked her
I knew my heart
when concrete met flesh
misjudged that bump and bicycles learned to fly
are tears really necessary? … walk it off
I knew my heart
when "one of the guys" was
pushing rumors down grapevines
thorns and all
and awkward silences when entering crowded rooms
"protect the brotherhood code"
I knew my heart
when men don't say
I love you
to other men
I knew my heart
when shirts vs skins
ribs and lanky arms and bird legs
and non-stop dogs barking with no respite; no solace
I knew my heart
when lights were out
and shapes are monstrous
calls go unanswered, nothing in the dark that isn't in the light
"grow up"
I knew my heart
Could decode the lies
my compass never pointed south

when I became my own cartographer, armorer and blacksmith
and I wrote my truth

*Originally published by Whisper and the Roar: A Feminist Literary
Collective (& outlaw poets swearing)*

Grapes on the Vine
Elijah R. Carney

I Knew My Name

I knew my name
when grown men
called me *honey*
fondled my braids
and pulled my
10-year-old body
—stiff with resistance—
onto their hard laps
I knew my name
when the male high school teacher
called me *sweetie*
and told me not to worry about
the 70 on my exam
because girls don't need
an A in chemistry
to be a good wife and mother
I knew my name
when the teenage boys
called me *ice queen*
cock tease
when I didn't want their
sloppy tongues down my throat
their rough hands
on my budding breasts
I knew my name
when men followed me
down the street
called me *bitch*
fucking dyke
when I wouldn't smile
or say 'thank you'

257

to their declarations
of lewd things
they would do to me
once we were alone
I knew my name
when my children
called me *mommy*
389 times a day
until I wanted to scream
all other identities
lost in a fugue state
of sleeplessness,
endless laundry
and dirty diapers
I knew my name
when male eyes
slid off like teflon
as they absently
called me *ma'am*
when I turned 50
let my hair go gray
chiming in that I reminded them
of their mothers
as if it were a compliment
I knew my name
when I trusted my eyes
to see my own truth clearly

and my voice
to speak it
and rejected those names
I did not choose for myself

Originally published by *Whisper and the Roar: A Feminist Literary Collective (& outlaw poets swearing)*

I Knew My Mistakes
Kristiana Reed

I knew my mistakes when they were emblazoned
across my chest, a red poker hot dress
you bought for me when I forgot your tea
or to arrange the flowers perfectly.

I knew my mistakes when both hello
and goodbye were pursed lips,
a cold shoulder in the sheets,
a clarion call of silence.

I knew my mistakes when you shared them
with our friends, your mother and mine,
a verbatim list of why you didn't have the time
to raise me an angel following in your wake.

I knew my mistakes when pity
felt more like love than kissing you
goodnight, lying in wait for you to finish
me – breakfast, lunch and dinner.

I knew my mistakes when I said I was leaving
and opened the door for you,
letting the useless escape from my bones
to join you with your suitcase and the dead.

Originally published by *Whisper and the Roar: A Feminist Literary Collective (& outlaw poets swearing)*

I Knew My Place
Marcia J. Weber

I knew my place when I was cooking
barefoot
scrambling to please
the indomitable hostess
fierce in a frazzled up-do
sizzling while he sat at ease.
I knew my place when I was chewing
my cheeks
cognizant of my inconsequence
biting back that biting retort
while they chewed conceited cud
confident of their pompous placement.
I knew my place when I was toiling
drudgery
forbidden from the boardroom
as I covered incompetence
silver coffee serviette
service with a smile.
I knew my place when I was massaging
his ego
and his member, crafting a pleasure cruise
dutiful and doting
at the expense of my own satisfaction.

I know my place when I am standing
strong
solid on my own two feet
above the clamoring fray
going my own way.

Originally published *by Whisper and the Roar: A Feminist Literary Collective (& outlaw poets swearing)*

Thread
Jharna Choudhury

Hand in Hand

with Rana Kelly, crystal x, Nicole Lyons, Sun Hesper
Jansen, Candice Louisa Daquin, and Lois Linkens
A Weyward Sisters Collaboration

Stand, a *nighean.*
Call the moon.
Bring your Wolves
With you.
Let down the flames of your hair.
The Great War
Has come again.
Rana Kelly

for sisters who never came home;
sisters shattered into constellations
over the Kewa rez, who whisper:
close your eyes
when you drive down
the turquoise trail,
breathe me in -
wear red.
crystal x

It is well within the fires
of burning words
and stolen wombs, ravaged,
we have birthed a beast.
Swaddled in the souls
of her mothers of fire
and maidens of ice,
she has been touched
with the wisdom of crones blazing,

and she will cast
her shadow upon the ashes
of their bones.
Nicole Lyons

Here in this circle where all love
is sacred, we flesh the flayed
in earth, clothe the nameless
in air, speak our truths
in fire, temper unseen blades
in water charged by the moon.
Lady of the Crossroads,
we stride in your light
hand in hand.
Sun Hesper Jansen

whether we lick the match
setting it soft against skin
or spill burning onto paper
where pyres witch the watcher
whether we lose the blood
of generations, spilt in gory hollow
controlled, buttoned up and swallowed
incomplete and brim with rage
still we endure, it is our way
women who survive do not
tear so much as scream
"you will not have me"
fierce throats bared
as if to dare, those weak
enough for conquering's foil
poor endeavored fail
whether we lick the match
to our own party of destruction

still we dance in flames
the woman phoenix
reborn
Candice Louisa Daquin

hail the harlot
and crown the courtesan,
she has seen seduction's beast
and let it swallow her.
let her tread its veins like footpaths
and sleep sound on its heart.
Lois Linkens

we stand shoulder to
shoulder
with our sisters
warrior women all
we draw down the moon
hold her firmly as our shield
our pens hammered not into
plowshares but sharpened swords
we will be silenced
no longer
our whispered chant of truth
strengthened in solidarity
the chorus of our voices
rising into a roar
Christine E. Ray

Nighean is Scottish Gaelic for "lass."

Rooting Up
Jharna Choudhury

Malevolent Melody

with Marcia J. Weber, Kindra M. Austin, Sarah Doughty,
Devika Mathur, and Laurie Wise

Your Urgency Pierced My Marrow
with vanilla milquetoast
pleadings
you spun a web
the envy of Arachne
smeared in syrupy cajolery –
I supped on hand-dipped flattery
your urgency pierced my marrow with flim flam
Marcia J. Weber

Dilly Dalliance Bound Me
Lavender dipped
indulgent tongue
dripped incantations,
salacious songs—
your abuse was tender
dilly dalliance bound me with feathers
Kindra M. Austin

The Honey You Gave
Those words were sweet as honey and I drank them down like
they were all for me. I fell for each one. But slowly, beneath my
rose-covered eyes, they soured.
And, piece by piece, you took all you wanted from me.
Sarah Doughty

Your Hands Are Stiff Wire
Cinnamon sticks plummeting
screeching lullaby with love and hunger,

a spasm spews on the back of an ant
the circle of disgust and disgust
my legs are broken, my arms are missing
yellow stingy archaic cry
ruffling touch,
you disappear like a swollen pollen grain
as I chop my hair, chop the hideous you.
Devika Mathur

Lies and Propaganda
Anything goes, according to your arrogant agenda
Gaslight fueled, devotion fooled
Poisonous thirst for possession
And domination obsession
Believing exemption from
Sugar coated sin
As long as you win
Sticks and stones broke my bones, your lies and propaganda
broke my spirit
Laurie Wise

No Longer Your Canvas
I throw out the bouquet of violets, saliva, red roses
you lay in empty contrition on our sheets of white linen
where I nurse the most recent bruises you have drawn with your
fists
once you are gone, I adorn myself in essential oils
bittersweet for truth
thyme for strength
rosemary for remembrance
though my left eye may be swollen shut
I have never seen more clearly

than I do as I walk out the door, hidden suitcases in hand
I will no longer be the canvas for your unholy rage
Christine E. Ray

Originally published by *Blood Into Ink: Warrior Voices of Survival*

At the Gates of Dawn

Georgianna Grentzenberg

I Am the Woman

I am the woman
your mother warned you about
the one whose darkness
was hidden below
sunny faux finish
of excellent manners
honor roll grades
my monster heart hidden
so well that no one noticed
me drowning
in my self-hate
I am the woman
who cut my teeth
on black leather
and handcuffs
control a requirement
for my release
I am the woman
with scrolls of black ink
symbols of resistance
of resilience
etched inch by inch
on my skin
a reclaiming of body
that was not always
home
I am the woman
who casually mentions
my ex-lovers
male and female

at the holiday table
pass the gravy, please
I am the woman
who finally started to speak
silence is *not* golden
truth is silver
and has wings

Originally published in *Composition of a Woman*

I Am the Woman

Marcia J. Weber

I am the woman
your mother warned you about
(let's face it she was *envious*)
I have long since lost my place
that musty corner
to which I was relegated
where nice girls sit quietly
legs crossed and demure.
                    (what point is there in that?)
I turn heads with my stride
I watch the eyes track my steps
though I pause not
in my progress.
                    do they tremble at my purpose?
                    or pause at my vibrant colored sheath?
I will not wait
until you deem me **old**
to wear red with purple
as I rock bold iconoclasm.
I am that version of herself
where holds are not barred
by convention or whalebone stays
                    crash those barriers my friend
                    be they concrete or glass.
I AM that woman you were warned about
who will challenge your ass*umptions
                    prove each wrong
                    geometrically, logically

I speak without being spoken to
(Imagine the gall!)
I have opinions
well thought and articulated
I will speak them
Still

Originally published by *Heretics, Lovers, and Madmen*

Imagination
Jharna Choudhury

I Am the Woman

Erin L. King

I am the woman
your mother warned you about.
You have a missing piece, he said
and he was right:
that piece was tolerance
for racist grandmothers
and gross jokes
told over tables of restraint.
That piece
that didn't think a six-year-old
should be a misogynist.
That piece
crying angry tears
when she showed up at my job
reprimanded me
for not putting Family first.
I am the woman
you see as unwhole
precisely because
I am whole.

Originally published by *Heretics, Lovers, and Madmen*

I Am the Woman
Dom Wynette

I'm the woman you're mother warned you about
The one people wince at what may come out of my mouth
I say what I want even at your grandmother's house
I might even slouch on her couch
Peep my reflection and take a selfie with my tongue out
Yea that's me.
The one she told you could never be a wife
Because I'm too obscene
Five foot nine, with half my height in my legs
Covered in ink, with clothes that compliment my curves
Your mom wants you with a tamable girl
Not one that makes her son beg
She only wants the BEST, I guess you're her whole world
But I'm the girl with a past life
A girl who wasted all her twenties being lost in the fast life
Two kids with two daddies, with no desire to have more
no grand-babies for her
I bet your mom thinks I'm a whore
She warned you about those baby mamas
She thinks my children diminish my worth
Well, I got news for that lady
I'm the wildest thing that's ever happened to you, baby
I might not have the prettiest history
Those are all facts, that's no mystery

But once you've had me, life without me is misery
I'm the best left, so its best you play it right
Before I leave you empty and let your mama tuck you in at night

Originally published by *Heretics, Lovers, and Madmen*

Crane

Elijah R, Carney

I Am the Woman
Basiliké Pappa

I am the woman your mother warned you about:
She and the other matriarchs exchanged recipes. Babies in
arms, children tugging at their sleeves. High pitched squealing.
The perfect detergent for spring cleaning.
I zoomed out.
Someone asked me something, I said 'what?' Then they
exchanged glances.
— Isn't the day hot, and could you beat the eggs?
—Sure, why not?
I beat the eggs and I was thinking the last time I did spring
cleaning must have been summer because it was hot. Then
someone came and brought me pot. That's how I missed a spot
on the window glasses.
I am the woman your mother warned you about:
When she told me 'when you get pregnant,' I said 'I'm not taking
any chances.'
'Son, she's cold. Chit-chat was like we spoke foreign languages.
I have a feeling she'll never bake a pie. She only paid attention
when I showed her the tear-free way of onion peeling.'
'What's worse, son, is she doesn't want kids. How selfish is this?
When a woman loves a man, she wants to multiply.'
'Lazy, uncaring, contemptuous of floral patterns — son, she's not
normal.'
Didn't she say these things to you?
Listen to her, they are all true.
Weather and wax for hardwood flooring
— baby, these politics are boring.
Scaling and steaming lake trout
— not for me. I'll dine out.

I'd rather read the half-truths of Karl Kraus
than spend my days in your house
with rubber gloves, scrubbing the cupboards
(vague displeasure in the suburbs.)
Brace yourself, here comes a shock:
I have no biological clock,
no desire to be your old lady
proud to be blessed with your baby.
I'm not normal; I confess:
can't sacrifice myself, I guess,
to win a place in your heart
(from loveless sex to sexless love.)
Which also means, I don't go 'oh!'
over the squareness of your jaw
and never fall in purple patches
when I swallow your discharges.
Tie me down, then play dog?
Think again, you missed a spot:
don't expect me to be loyal.
What can I say? I'm not normal.
I am the woman your mother warned you about,
the greatest enemy that prowls around.
Why don't you find someone else to bother?
Run home now, to your mother.

Originally published by *Heretics, Lovers, and Madmen*

I Am the Woman

Candice Louisa Daquin

I am the girl who was never the child
Seen too much, been too much, defiled and reviled
Stains the inside, halts growth, behind your eyes too many
images
Fitful in shade, don't know how to make, a real version of me
Seen so many attempts, the fakes and the frauds when do you
Grow up to be? A woman?
Lying in your arms, purging in the bathroom, lies upon lies
Pain begets pain, begets strength and illusion, which pill to take?
Smoking away the shame, nothing powerful enough to name
We stay without label to avoid burden of claim, no baby, no
womb
Take the real out, leave the fake and to the core rotten
When do you grow up to be? A woman?
After all is said and done, masturbation, rape, incest, are not the
tropes
Of this girl, she may not have much left, but within her lies a
seed
You cannot remove, nor discount, even though you've tried
mightily
She eats herself inside out, what returns is born from within the
husk
A woman at last, not a girl, not a sin, despite what her mother
may have said
She's here to stay, despite herself and your best attempt
Get used to it.

Originally published by *Heretics, Lovers, and Madmen*

I Am the Woman

Mandy Kocsis

I am the Woman
Your Mother never thought of
A Frankenstein monster
Stitched together with trauma & tears
Holding a Darkness; my greatest strength
The one who'll take the bullet
And annihilate the shooter
In one fell sweep
I am the Woman
Who bleeds in truthful ink
Who found her voice
After nights spent drowned in blood
Who clawed her way back to life
When there wasn't much worth living for
Who cries each night
Over the graves inside my soul
I am the Woman who holds on
When everyone lets go
A Woman your mother wouldn't know
I'm the Woman who survives.

Originally published by *Heretics, Lovers, and Madmen*

I Am the Woman

Susan M. Conway

I am the woman your mother warned you about; because my feminism threatens her existence.

I am the woman your mother warned you about; because she didn't say YES to the invite, the open door, the unlocked gate.

She stayed in the panic room of her fear, smashing the glass of her fire alarm psyche, ripping herself to shreds on the inside every night as she lay next to a man who barely even acknowledged her existence anymore, and waking in the morning to put everyone together, even though she was completely shattered.

I am the woman your mother warned you about; because my feminism is rambunctious, a lion's head, mouth open, teeth bared, soul too… too… too much to process, too big for my body, so I let her breathe, and see the light of day before we go deep again; too loud so I am shunned and a warning label slapped on my too much body, by other women, that found comfort in the wasteland of societal conformity.

I am the woman your mother warned you about; because it would be a crime most heinous and foul to have her own child celebrate his or her own bodies, to move freely in this world, to take up as much space as they wanted unapologetically, to teach others to do the same, and to go to war with those who sought to shame.

I am the woman your mother warned you about; because the big teeth and the loud roar of her trauma growls gravel down her throat, the roots deep shame in her sacral chakra weep, 'I can't, I am a woman, my period is disgusting, my body is a sinful temptress, my intellect is problematic, my ambition is wasted on my gender, I am not worth equal pay, and because it is shameful and gross to be a woman, I take this in as my truth, I AM SHAMEFUL, AND GROSS, AND UNWORTHY.

I can't, because I am a woman, and I am beholden to my husband. He paid the bills while I stayed home and cared for the children, the way it is supposed to be- right? Right?

I can't question, because I am a woman and I feel too deeply, I am far too sensitive, I just need to get over it, so I must never dig too deep. The ache begins when I steal a peek at freedom from this self-imposed prison sentence, and it won't go away until I am two bottles deep in wine, while everyone is asleep and I am falling… apart. I am my own jailer and I hate myself for it, and I hate myself because the world hates me and they have told me my entire life, at every turn, it is everywhere and in everything, being a woman is an abomination, loving your body makes you a slut, loving pleasure makes you a whore, not always having it together makes you a hideous mess, breaking down is interpreted as you being susceptible and weak, being drunk means you had it coming to you, walking down the street with breasts and a vagina means you were asking for it. It isn't safe. It isn't safe. It isn't safe.'

I know, Sister. I know it isn't safe, out there. Hell, we aren't even safe in our own homes. Nothing is ever a sure bet, really. But, I am willing to assume the risk if the reward is being stripped of every label the collective THEY placed on us. I will go to war for you even though you raised your sons to name me, cage me, and view my feminism as wicked.

I know what fear looks like from all angles, as I have been ravaged by many treacherous men and women. It changes you, you know that.

I know you know that. Our body is a fire alarm, all triggered and shit. We carry our keys like blades between our fingers in open public places, we have rules of engagement, don't make direct eye contact, buddy system, don't wear low cut shirts, don't wear tight pants, we can't wear dressed-up drives the menfolk crazy and they no longer are able to reasons with the head in their shoulders, if you do you're asking for it, you had it coming to you, they were just having a little fun, smile more, especially after they rape you, also say thank you, you don't get to be a disaster when they're finished with the erased-used-societally ruled pages-of our body, we gotta... keep it classy-you know?

I know...

And, I know that you know.

And whereas, I can understand and empathize with your fear; I must tell you that what you are calling logic, is actually toxicity. What you are calling protection, is actually fear projection. What you are calling other women who chose to leave the prison of their trauma and shame, and lead lives ferociously defending and compelling women to do the same- it makes you worse than the patriarchal system put in place to keep us in their wounded perspectives, in OUR PLACE.

There is a reason your mother warned you about women like me, and none of them were made with a sound mind and body.

We all get muddied, no matter the gender. Statistics show that more women than men fall victim to assault. It doesn't make the thing that happened irrelevant, lesser than in any way, shape, or form, and it doesn't mean that we, as women, don't have a long way to go in regard to raising our young men and even our partners to be feminists as well-proud of their bodies, outspoken about wrong doings and injustices, activists and advocates of healing and its power, sharing the things that hold our hearts prisoner, breaking up with this idea that we must police our humanity Allow society to. We all have much to learn, ladies; we have so much to unearth and to become from.

Blessed Be.

Originally published by *Heretics, Lovers, and Madmen*

I Am the Woman

Lynn Devora-McNabb

I am the woman
your mother warned you about.
The hushed voice
pretending everything was fine
telling me not to speak
removing the words from my throat
replacing them with self-hatred
creating the person I was becoming.
I am the woman
your mother warned you about.
The flash of fear
when my heart would stop
and veins would clog with ice
snapping me into an action
that only sometimes kept me safe
creating the person I was becoming.
I am the woman
your mother warned you about.
The silent screams
edges of a blade
sharpness of pain past
drawing blood that welled
slowly falling like tears
creating the person I was becoming.
I am the woman
your mother warned you about.
The confusion, the anger
helplessness of feeling
frozen in place with no way out

doors, windows bolted shut
imprisoned in a life of degradation
creating the person I was becoming.
I am the woman
your mother warned you about.
The explosion of awareness
a split second when time stood still
gasoline poured over a carefully sculpted life
a single lit match burning it all down
raking through the remains
creating the person I was becoming.
I am the woman
your mother warned you about.
The piece of fire-hardened clay
lovingly softened and molded
end results not important
only the process of
shaping and reshaping
creating the person I am becoming.
I am the woman
your mother warned you about.
The warmth and tenderness
long fought, scraping and clawing acceptance of self
softness of my body
connecting with hers
quietly spoken words of love
creating the person I am becoming.
I am the woman
your mother warned you about.
The dichotomy, the contradiction
the paradox of emotions conceived in
a multitude of experiences.
The hurt, the sorrow, the pain

nestled among an ever growing expanse of love, joy, and
laughter
changing the person I was into the person I am,
the woman your mother warned you about.

Originally published by *Heretics, Lovers, and Madmen*

Picasso's Head of a Woman
Jharna Choudhury

I Am the Woman
Kristiana Reed

I am the woman
your mother warned you about;
fire-breathing, Jolene auburn,
cradled by the night
and the ever waning moon
melting like candle wax
into my palms.
I am the woman
too many men have kept
secret and hidden;
I spent too long
looking at love
through the underside
of a glass bottomed boat
swallowing seawater,
bitter and sweet.
I am the woman
who blossomed beneath
the heavy thud of fists;
who learned to lie
better than love
and wear scorn in
my half-chewed smile.
I am the woman
your mother warned you about
because in my eyes
she sees her own.

Originally published by *Heretics, Lovers, and Madmen*

I Am the Woman

Kindra M. Austin

She is me—
the woman your mother warned you about
when your childish hands declared they were a man's
and left hers empty to grieve.
I am the one who won't love you through
alcoholic bursts of abuse. I won't chew on
belittlement flavored bubblegum and just be
happy
you
acknowledged me.
I am not the one to love you
unconditionally;
and I won't be the light you reach for when you've
gone and done it,
again.
I'd rather eat the stars and leave us all in
darkness.
I am the woman your mother warned you about
when your infidelity slipped out of your pants and into
another's mouth.
I am the woman your mother warned you about
when you pressed your teeth against my cheek
and snarled.
I am the woman your mother warned you about, and I'll
be damned
if your daughter isn't, too.

Originally published by *Heretics, Lovers, and Madmen*

I Am the Woman
Sarah Doughty

Sometimes, I've seen the questions in your eyes. The ones that wonder what happened when the moon hung high in the night, illuminating the monster below. The ones that try to make sense of the way I managed to navigate through my adolescence with so much baggage dragging me down. The ones that ponder when you think I'm not paying attention— the ones that scrutinize just what went on in the darkness all those nights. You see, I am the woman that managed to find my way out of hell. I am the woman that battles those demons non-stop while also trying to live in the present. I am the broken woman. The battered woman. The defaced. The defiled. The rotten. I am the woman your mother warned you about.

Originally published on *Heretics, Lovers, and Madmen*

I Am the Woman

K. Bailey Ressel

I am the woman they
tried to silence with expectations
of perfect beauty
questionable truths wrapped
in family tradition
bound in
shame.
I am the authentic
legacy of cheaters, liars,
abusers, addicts–
of parental neglect, the
parentified child,
the blackest
sheep.
I am the breaker
of hearts and silence
chains and chance, watch
as I burn in effigy
everything meant
to break my
voice.

Originally published by *Heretics, Lovers, and Madmen*

I Am the Woman

Rachael Z. Ikins

I'm the child you locked in.
Every afternoon and every Saturday morning. The child you said
was fat, whose food you took away, who served you dessert but
wasn't allowed to lick the spoon.
I was that too-blonde, too-good, girl who was too afraid to touch
Down There. Using allowance on 10 candy bars at a time, I'm
the girl who got high.
Eating them one after another in a dim room, a sunny after-
school afternoon, chocolate high. I never learned to vomit.
I am the woman who held you when you were dying. The
woman who straddled the recliner where you lay,
your face yellow as mustard in your dying,
as you leaked blood from skin too thin to contain it,
I am the woman who said, "No! You will not take my mother out
of this house." You would've died screaming in agony in an
ambulance, and for what? Because staff worried about a
lawsuit? I guarded you, stood while my brother hid in the
kitchen.
Later I heard an owl pair, that frigid December moonrise. I ran
inside with my dogs, hollering, "Mom, mom! Owls!"
You looked at me one last time, the pull of the bond between us
almost stronger than death. I felt useless and small.
Later still. Dogs barking—you had flown with them.
I am the woman who sat with you after, gently unclenched your
hand to remove your rings, careful to give my brother the
birthstone blue you got when he arrived. The center of your thin
palm still holding small heat.
I am that woman. Your only daughter.
Forgiveness is not always possible, but I have no regrets when I

think back to that night four years ago. You gave me my life. I had to learn to fight to live it.

Originally published by *Heretics, Lovers, and Madmen*

The Weeping Woman
Jharna Choudhury

Originally published in *Through The Looking Glass: Reflecting on Madness and Chaos Within*

The Beauty Myth

beauty beholds me
finds me wanting…
cringes
at lack
of adherence
to carved commandments
lay down
in pages of glossy
fashion magazines
self-appointed
arbitrators
of what
making an effort
looks like
to what I *should*
aspire

my hair
too thin
too gray
too badly (self) cut

　　　　　do you even own a brush or comb?!

skin lined
bare
pallid except
where it is blotchy
blotchy except
where it is pallid
no mascara

lip liner
concealer to be
found

we've seen ghosts with more color
than you
sighs
exasperated
at today's ensemble-
sweatpants
(dark gray? navy? black?)
shapeless
oversized sweatshirt
(mostly unstained)
worn fleece-lined
clogs
anime socks
adding unexpected spot of color
of whimsy

seriously, you leave the house in that?!
putting a bra on is NOT 'dressing up'

beauty beholds me
finds me wanting. . .

if only
I cared

Weight

Jharna Choudhury

Tuesday Morning Serenade

slow morning wake
interrupted
unexpected serenade
Pretty Woman
sung slightly
off-key with
confident bravado
only a stranger
wandering by an
open window
while wearing
headphones
can muster
another might
imagine it
a command
performance
meant for only
my ears
but I no longer
hold illusions
of 'pretty'
'pretty' belongs
to smooth
soft cheeks
bloomed with youth
the ribboned road
stretched out
smoothly before
bright eyes
promising 2 am

whispered ardor
more years ahead
than behind
I have weathered
into 'interesting'
cracked sidewalk
each line
each imperfection
holding
a story
to tell

Daisy
Elijah R. Carney

About the Author

Christine E. Ray (She/Her) lives outside of Philadelphia, Pennsylvania. A former Managing Editor of Sudden Denouement Publications, she co-founded Indie Blu(e) Publishing with Kindra M. Austin in September 2018. Ray is author of *Composition of a Woman* and *The Myths of Girlhood*. Her writing has also been featured in *But You Don't Look Sick: The Real Life Adventures of Fibro Bitches, Lupus Warriors, and other Superheroes Battling Invisible Illness*, *Through The Looking Glass: Reflecting on Madness and Chaos Within*, *As The World Burns: Writers and Artists Reflect on a World Gone Mad*, *SMITTEN: This Is What Love Looks Like*, *We Will Not Be Silenced: The Lived Experience of Sexual Harassment and Sexual Assault Told Powerfully*

Through Poetry, Prose, Essay, and Art, Anthology Volume I: Writings from the Sudden Denouement Literary Collective, Swear to Me (Nicholas Gagnier), and *All the Lonely People* (Nicholas Gagnier).

Christine is a passionate fiber artist who has rarely met a craft supply she doesn't like or a pattern she can't alter. Currently yarn obsessed, over the decades she has learned to knit, crochet, quilt, weave, bead, and has dabbled in mixed media. Christine doesn't have a spinning wheel... yet.

Hydrangea

Elijah R. Carney

About the Collaborators

Kindra M. Austin is a poet and gothic fiction author from Mid-Michigan. She co-founded Indie Blu(e) Publishing with Christine E. Ray in 2018. Her published works include two novels, (*The Black Naught* and *The Killing Holiday*), and six books of poetry (*Constant Muses*, *TWELVE*, *All the Beginnings of Everything*, *Heavy Mental*, *I Am a War*, and *Little Book of Blackness*). It's her dream to open a bookstore/craft beer bar. She will call it, *Get Lit*. You can follow Kindra M. Austin on Instagram: @gothic.poser

Elijah R. Carney was born and raised in the Philadelphia area. He received his photography degree from Delaware County Community College in 2023. Elijah is an aspiring photographer who enjoys music and video games.

I am **Jharna Choudhury**. I have been carrying a zoo on my back, and I live in a carnivorous home. When my animals fight inside me, I have to constantly type it out, until they calm down. Otherwise, I get my fabric, thread and needle; make knots to tie them up. I also release the hounds, bears, hyenas, and vicious snakes in the black (back) waters of my mind. My creative writing has been published in *Muse India*, *The Little Journal of Northeast India*, Spillwords, *SETU*, *Pine Cone Review*, *The Assam Tribune*, *The Sentinel*, and forthcoming in *Ethelzine*. My poetry has found a home in the anthologies: *Unsent Letters: From the South Asian Diaspora* (2021), *Through the Looking Glass: Reflecting on Madness and Chaos Within* (2021), *But You Don't Look Sick: The Real Life Adventures of Fibro Bitches, Lupus Warriors, and other Superheroes Battling Invisible Illness* (2021), *Pause and Pen: Whispers of the Soul* (2021), *Paradise on Earth* (Vol II) (2022), *The Body of Memories* (2022), *Pixie Dust and All Things Magical* (2022), and *Poetry on a Plate with Spicy Mango Pickle* (2022). I have embroidered the book cover design of an Assamese short story collection, *Champawatir Na-kai Xajaa Gharkhon* (2022). Instagram @_embroidery_stories_

Ward Clever writes, sings, paints and dreams from his rose garden in upstate New York.

Susan M. Conway pushes boundaries in her writing, fearlessly tackling a range of controversial subjects with unapologetic honesty. Her works with Indie Blu(e) Publishing and her personal blogs explore themes such as addiction, mental illness, and unconventional relationships, unearthing the multifaceted layers of human experiences that are often brushed under the rug. Conway's writing style is characterized by its rawness and emotional intensity. She fearlessly exposes the raw emotions and vulnerabilities of herself and characters, inviting readers into their inner worlds with unflinching authenticity. Through her storytelling, she aims to challenge societal taboos, provoke empathy, and foster a greater understanding of the diverse human experiences that exist in the world. Beyond her writing, Conway is an advocate for social change and equality. She actively supports organizations and individuals that promote the rights and well-being of marginalized communities, using her platform to amplify their voices and raise awareness about their struggles. Susan M. Conway's work is undeniably powerful and thought-provoking. With her daring exploration of taboo subjects and her unwavering commitment to destigmatizing marginalized communities and pushing societal boundaries, Conway continues to challenge readers, confront societal norms, and shed light on the often silenced stories of those on the fringes of society. You can find her on: Facebook: @AuthorSusanConway

Born in Europe, **Candice Louisa Daquin** is of Sephardi French/ Egyptian descent. Daquin was the Publishing Director at the U.S. Embassy (London) before becoming a Psychotherapist. Daquin is Senior Editor at Indie Blu(e) Publishing, a feminist micro-press and Editorial Partner with Raw Earth Ink. She's also Writer-in-Residence for *Borderless Journal*, Editor of Poetry & Art for *The Pine Cone Review* and Poetry Editor for *Parcham Literary Magazine*. Daquin's own poetic work takes its form from the confessional women poets of the 20th century as well as queer authors writing from the 1950's onward. Her career(s) teaching critical thinking and practicing as a psychotherapist have heavily influenced her writing. As a queer woman of mixed ethnicity and passionate feminist beliefs concerning equality, Daquin's poetry is her body of evidence.

Lynn Devora-McNabb is a longtime writer and educator. She lives on an island in the Pacific Northwest with her wife, their three dogs, and two cats. She loves reading, writing, walking the beach, and filling her wife's pockets with heart rocks.

Sarah Doughty is a Smashwords Most Downloaded Author of fiction and poetry, including a contributor to publications online and in print, including *We Will Not Be Silenced*, and *Crown Anthologies*. As a survivor, Sarah writes to cope with her complex PTSD. She lives in Indiana with her family.

Michael Erickson is a small-time writer and blogger. Between teaching and raising two rambunctious kids he finds time to write poetry, prose, and short stories. He thoroughly enjoyed writing for *Go Dog Go Cafe* as a guest barista for the last few years and has his own writing blog showcasing many poems and short stories. You can read more of his writing on Wordpress at The Ink Owl

Rachel Finch originally started using poetry as a way to accurately express herself after a number of traumatic experiences in her young life. She is the founder of Bruised But Not Broken which was started with the purpose to raise awareness of abuse and provide a place of comfort and support throughout the healing process. She believes that it was with the support of this community that she was able to recover from sexual abuse and move towards healing mind, body and soul. Rachel Finch is the author of *A Sparrow Stirs its Wings*, *Conversations with my Higher Self*, and *I am draped in Soul; it is a nakedness*. Her work has also been published in the anthologies *We Will Not Be Silenced*, *As the World Burns*, and *Smitten*.

Devereaux Frazier is a published poet and writer, contributor to *Blood Into Ink*, Guest Barista for *Go Dog Go Cafe*. His work has also been featured on *SpillWords.com*, where he was nominated for the May Publication of the Month in 2017. You can also find him published in *Literary Arts Review* and *Teen Ink*, the latter of which published his work in their monthly magazine in 2016.

Stephen Fuller is thrilled to be included in this collection of poetry alongside some of the good people he has met on his writing journey over the last 6 years. He is equally astonished by how prolific and smooth his collaborations with Christine have been and might say that on any given day they share a poetic mind. Today, Stephen writes less after a life transformation of epic proportions: divorce, retirement, move, new job in a new profession and all the excitement those changes entail; friendships, relationships, dogs, cats, and lots of beautiful land in the Driftless area of Wisconsin. No complaints, just a smile for how life finally turns when you stare down the demons with the love and support of family and friends.

Nicholas Gagnier is the author of several books, including *The Book of Death* series and *Eidetica*. He lives in Ottawa with his family and circus of a dogs.

Georgianna Grentzenberg has been active in the arts in the Philadelphia area for over 40 years. She attended the Pennsylvania Academy of the Fine Arts from 1978-1982. She has shown in many juried, and one person exhibitions. Her primary work takes the form of fantastical visions and gardens done in ink and colored pencil.

Iulia Halatz is a city councilor, entrepreneur, editor, and writer who believes that doing what one does best is the best way to accomplish what one wants. Without her storytelling abilities, she would have been an ordinary high school teacher in Bucharest. For her and her students, teaching is a real-time narrative experience, so it comes naturally. Her storytelling skills led her into the political process after she wrote a terrific cover letter for a "Women in Politics" event. As a genuine woman in politics striving to improve, she works on community projects with local organizations, interest groups, and businesses. She invented the word "workwomanship" to figuratively depict the problems and efforts involved in this vocation. She has been writing for international publications, and some of her poems have been included in the *Sudden Denouement Anthology Volume 1*. She is of the opinion that "Writing can change lives, but good writing has the Midas touch". Without her storytelling cloak, she is just an enthusiastic, strong-willed, hard-working adventure seeker, energetic reader, vicarious traveler, and passionate cyclist.

Saide Harb-Ranero's writing journey began as a pre-teen, sitting in her room writing daily in her diary. Born in Lebanon, she is a survivor of a civil war who lived in an underground shelter for a year. Fluent in both Arabic and French, she taught herself English by listening to Alanis Morissette in the 90's and translating song lyrics to keep her writing private. The author of *Not a Victim* now shares her writing publicly in hopes of giving others comfort and support. Read more at: https://www.saideharbranero.com/

Quatrina Hosain is a Pakistani journalist who writes verse when she is enraged and then deletes it all. This is her first foray into sharing her dark thoughts. She graduated from Mount Holyoke College in 1987 and immediately went into mainstream journalism on her return to Pakistan. She has worked for several news organizations, including Agence France Presse. She covered the war in Sri Lanka and unrest in Bangladesh in the 1990s, becoming Pakistan's first woman war correspondent. She has been the editor of a national newspaper and anchored television news programs for several years. She has interviewed several heads of state from around the world. During an unplanned hiatus from journalism, she returned to her first love of rescuing animals and running an animal shelter. She also remains deeply involved in improving legislation for animal rights. For the past 15 years, she has focused on tracking terrorist and extremist ideologies and worked on reclaiming space conceded over the years. She trains police officers, anti-terrorist court prosecutors and government officials in strategic communications pertaining to terrorism and violent extremism. She also develops and deploys counter violent extremism campaigns. Much of her personal writing is drawn from the hatred and hostility towards women promoted by extremist organizations. She currently lives with her 15 rescue cats and two dogs and divides her time between Karachi and Islamabad. Someday, she hopes to finish writing her book on the Mughul queen, Empress Nurjehan.

Rachael Z. Ikins followed her pen into the forest as a child. As with Gretel in the Grimm Brothers' tale, a wicked witch forced her to reroute through valleys so dark she doubted the existence of the sun at times. A fabulous wizard held her heart in his hand. They fell in love. He urged her to release poetry from her soul. She lost everything before she finally understood her truth: write like a motherfucker, write or die. For poetry was the constant through all storms, the beloved she refused to relinquish. She won some prizes, published in journals and then books. When last seen, Ikins was feeding pickled jalapeños to a large dragon perched on the roof of her house—a dragon who bestowed her name upon Ikins's cat. Sister souls of fire and passion.

Sun Hesper Jansen (she/they) is a poet, writer, and artist from Madison, Wisconsin, who works in the darker genres of fantasy, science fiction, and magical realism. Her collection of poetry and artwork, *Fairy of Disenchantment*, was published in 2023 by Indie Blu(e) Publishing, and she blogs as literary therapy for Multiple Sclerosis on WordPress at Fairy of Disenchantment.

Her work has appeared in *The Winged Moon Magazine*, *The Chamber Magazine*, and the Indie Blu(e) Publishing anthologies *As the World Burns: Writers and Artists Reflect on a World Gone Mad*, and *But You Don't Look Sick: The Real Life Adventures of Fibro Bitches, Lupus Warriors, and Other Superheroes Battling Invisible Illness*. You can find her on Instagram @sunhesper.

Rana Kelly was born and raised in the Deep South and now lives in the Southwestern desert, usually praying for rain. She published her first poem during childhood and has since published many more works, including a novel, creative nonfiction and personal essays in varied literary magazines and independent presses. She is enamored of pre-Christian mythology and pulls inspiration from it often. She dreams of finishing a proper Gothic before she escapes the mortal toil.

Erin L. King loves writing emotionally evocative poetry, designing jewelry and other objects, and eating Indian food. She lives with an ornery cat in suburban Philadelphia.

Mandy Kocsis is a poet with a dark soul and a commitment to healing. Determined to be more than the nightmares she's lived, she bleeds her darkness into beauty and gives it to the world. The author of "Soul Survivor" also has an affinity for all things Wonderland and magic. She knows there is light in the darkness, if only one knows where to look. Born and raised in Detroit, Michigan, Mandy currently resides with her family in southern Indiana.

Aakriti Kuntal is a poet, writer, and visual artist whose work has been published in *The Night Heron Barks*, *Silver Birch Press*, *Selcouth Station*, and *Poetry at Sangam* among others. She was awarded the Reuel International Prize 2017, shortlisted for the RL Poetry Award 2018, and nominated for the Best of the Net.

John W. Leys was first moved to write song lyrics after being introduced to the Beatles and Bob Dylan when he was a teenager. A chance encounter with a radioactive fountain pen turned him into a ukulele playing poet, a curse he's had to live with for decades The greatest influences on his poetry have been Lord Byron, Leonard Cohen, Allen Ginsberg, Bob Dylan, Catullus, Erica Jong, and a chemical imbalance in his brain. John's first poetry collection, *The Darkness of his Dreams*, was published in 2019. *Whispers of a One-Eyed Raven: Mythological Poetry* and *When the Banshee Howls and other poems* followed over the next few years. He's also been published in anthologies from Indie

Blu(e) Publishing, one of which he helped edit. He often wonders, in the third person, if anyone reads these author bios, or if he's just wasting his time trying to be clever. When not writing poetry, John can usually be found playing one of his many ukuleles or feeding the crows & ravens in the park.

Lois Linkens currently lives in Hull, England. She is working on doctoral research on indeterminacy in Romantic poetry and enjoys writing poetry and short stories.

Nicole Lyons is a force of nature disguised as a writer, a social activist, a voice for the downtrodden, and a powerful poet with a delicate touch. She is an award-winning poet and bestselling published author. Her work has been featured on CBC Books as well as numerous online magazines and print anthologies. Nicole was inducted into The Mental Health Writer's Guild in 2015 for her work on The Lithium Chronicles, Psych Central, The Mighty, and the International Bipolar Foundation. In her free time, Nicole volunteers as a speaker and event coordinator with a Canadian non-profit that focuses on suicide awareness and prevention in children and teens. She lives a good life in beautiful British Columbia with her brilliant daughters and an amazing husband. From a sunny porch in beautiful British Columbia, Nicole is enjoying a glass of wine and working on her next collection of poetry.
To connect with Nicole on social media, follow her:
Facebook & Instagram: @nicolelyonspoetry
Twitter: @nicolelyonspoet
thelithiumchronicles.org

The writing of Indie author **Jamie Lynn Martin**, is as raw and diverse as the culture of her hometown, New Orleans, LA. At age 7, Jamie began writing as a therapeutic outlet to express the emotions locked within. Even now she turns to ink for self-medicating. In addition to Jamie's upcoming book of poetry and prose, her words have been featured in Cult Magazine, *We Will Not Be Silenced: The Lived Experience of Sexual Harassment and Sexual Assault Told Powerfully Through Poetry, Prose, Essay, and Art*, and all across social media.

Devika Mathur is a bilingual poet who resides in India and is the author of *Crimson Skins*. Her work has also been published in *Madras Courier, Kitaab.org, Selcouth Station, Modern Literature, Indian Review, Whisper and the Roar*, and *Sudden Denouement Literary Collective*, to name a few. She has written for more than 40 journals and loves to share similar thoughts through her initiative; *Olive skins- a virtual platform for all surrealist writers*. She was recently a part of the '*Best of Mad Swirl*' anthology and has work included in the astounding anthology *BymePoetica vol 2*., as well as, *All the Lonely People*. She loves to express her thoughts through her WordPress blog, My Valiant Soul

Nathan McCool is the author of the poetry collections *Rejectamenta* and The Fall of Petals. His writing has also appeared in *Sudden Denouement Anthology Volume 1* and *Swear to Me*.

Jack Neece is a passionate woman who wishes to open eyes as well as hearts. Her writing has always been the salve that heals the wounds of her past. She hopes the same experience is had by those that read her work. Throughout her life Jack experienced a lot of trauma and uses this as a platform to reach out to others. Through her work and with her voice she is doing what she can to make the world a better place.

Allister Nelson is a 30-something poet and author.

S. K. Nicholas is a student of fine art, but over the years has become a disciple of literature. The author of three journals, titled *A Journal for Damned Lovers*, and a work of fiction, *X and I: A Novel*, he currently resides in England and spends his time working through a never ending to-do list.

Jesica Nodarse is a Cuban-born immigrant living in Florida, with her husband and children. A powerful writer and poet, an intense and driven woman, Jesica offers her unique perspective in today's world and empowers her friends and colleagues with passion and grace. Jesica can be found on Facebook @heathenwordsmith & Instagram at @jesicanodarse

An **OldePunk** trying to make sense of what I see and hear and think and feel. Words pulled from the ether. Sanely mad, mildly insane. Introverted agoraphobic explorer. Hockey, gaming and food junkie (snob).

Basiliké Pappa lives in Greece. She is a translator and copy editor, and writes poetry and prose in both Greek and English. Her work can be found in *Dark Passions Magazine, Heron Tree, Carmina Magazine, Ubu., Sledgehammer Lit, Glitchwords,* and other journals, as well as in the anthologies *Hidden in Childhood* (Literary Revelations, 2023), *Wounds I Healed: The Poetry of Strong Women* (Experiments in Fiction, 2022) and *Shaping Water: Erotic Haiku and Tanka* (Moth Orchid Press, 2022).

Kristiana Reed (she/her) is a bisexual writer and the Editor in Chief for *Free Verse Revolution*, a literary & arts magazine. Reed often explores the body, illness, addiction recovery and womanhood through the natural world and written portraiture.

Zelda Reville is a writer whose poetry has been published previously in *The Wire's Dream* and *No Extra Words*. Their writing is centered around explorations of fleeting beauty and the subconscious.

K. Bailey Ressel is a Pushcart Prize Nominee with several published fiction, non-fiction, poetry, and audio pieces in online and print journals and anthologies. She currently plays guitar and writes songs with her husband. They live in Pennsylvania with two dogs and two cats.

Megha Sood is an Award-winning Asian American Poet, Editor, and Literary Activist from New Jersey, USA. She is a Literary Partner with *"Life in Quarantine"*, at Stanford University. Member of *National League of American Pen Women* (NLAPW), *Women's National Book Association,* and *United Nations Association-US Chapter*. She is the recipient of the 2021 Poet Fellowship from MVICW (Martha's Vineyard Institute of Creating Writing), a 2022 mini-grant for Kundiman, a 2020 National Level Winner for the Poetry Matters Project, and a Four-Time State Level Winner for NAMI NJ Dara Axelrod Poetry Award. Her works have been nominated for Pushcart and Best of Net. She is an Associate Editor for the literary journals *Mookychick* (UK) and Brownstone Poets (USA). Author of Chapbook (*My Body is Not an Apology*, Finishing Line Press, 2021) and Full Length (*My Body Lives Like a Threat*, FlowerSongPress, 2022). Her widely anthologized poems, essays, and other works talk about her experience as a first-generation immigrant and woman of color. Her co-edited anthology and a few selected poems *The Medusa Project* has been selected as a digital payload to be sent to the moon in 2024 as part of the historical *LunarCodex Project* in collaboration with NASA/SpaceX. Find her at https://linktr.ee/meghasood

Eric Syrdal is a poet and author of the novel *Pantheon*. He's an avid gamer and Sci-Fi enthusiast. He enjoys reading science fiction and fantasy literature and spends a great deal of his writing time focused in those genres. He is a romantic at heart. His work usually contains elements of the supernatural and fantastic along with potent female voices and archetypes.

crystal x lives and writes in the southwest.

Marcia J. Weber dreamt of becoming a writer as a child. That dream was tabled as she pursued a career, family life and motherhood. In the midst of a life changing squall, writing became her life raft. She has been published in *The Poetic Bond VII* and *VIII*, *Orion Magazine*, *Writings from Sudden Denouement Literary Collective*, *We Will Not Be Silenced*, *As The World Burns*, and electronically on *Spillwords*. She writes as Aurora Phoenix at Insights from "Inside".

Bob Wertzler is retired from nearly twenty years in the mental health field both in California and Arizona. There are times the title, "Recovering Therapist," seems to fit. In 2006 Bob retired (again) to move to western North Carolina to help and become the primary caregiver for his father who had developed Dementia. Before all that, there was much work at various times as a soldier (US Army 196770), community organizer, cab driver, welfare case worker, wooden toy maker, carpenter, warehouse worker, among other things. He relates to a line in a Grateful Dead song, "What a long, strange trip it's been" But there is a life beyond work and keeping fed, clothed, and sheltered, and for him that has been much involved with reading, writing, and listening. He learned to read and love books from his father reading to him at bedtime and gradually transitioning to Bob doing the reading. It was not generally those things called "children's books" that he remembers most, although there must have been some. Instead, his sharpest memories are of the works of Jules Verne, Robert Louis Stevenson (what six-year- old boy wouldn't want to meet a real pirate like Long John Silver?), Robert Heinlein, Louis Carroll, Edgar Allan Poe, Ernest Hemingway (age seven, devouring The Old Man And The Sea), and many others. Nothing school presented could hold a candle to those storytellers. Bob credits whatever skill he has as a writer to those experiences and those examples absorbed as if by osmosis. One more favorite, this, from Bob Dylan: "he not busy being born is busy dying."

His recently published poetry collection, *The Comment Poems* is available at Lulu in paperback and eBook formats.

Connect with Bob online:
Wordpress: CABBAGESANDKINGS524
Facebook:
https://www.facebook.com/profile.php?id=100009494928086
LinkedIn: https://www.linkedin.com/in/robert-wertzler-548b97b7/

Laurie Wise resides in the Pacific Northwest, where she gardens, rescues dogs, and writes poetry and prose. She finds her inspiration stumbling through the darkness, searching for signs of life. Wise has been published in several anthologies, including *Darker Objects*, *Sudden Denouement Anthology Volume 1*, *All the Lonely People*, *Swear to Me* and *We Will Not Be Silenced*. Her essays on mental health and chronic pain have been featured in *The Mighty*. Laurie has been a member of on-line literary groups, Blood into Ink, Whisper and the Roar and Sudden Denouement Literary Collective.

Most pieces you read from **Dom Wynette** are fragments of her in breadcrumb poems and rants, that are begging her readers to follow the trail to her soul. As a stage four cancer survivor, the mother of four is most recognized for her transparency through her words, she is also unafraid to go against the grain to release her thoughts. Learn more at DomTheBlogger.com

Other Indie Blu(e) Publishing Titles You Might Enjoy

COMPOSITION OF A WOMAN

CHRISTINE E RAY

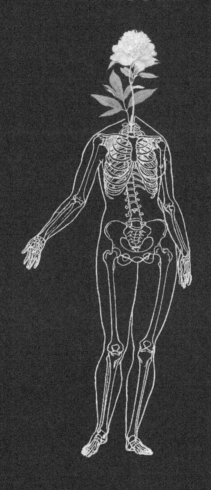

THE MYTHS OF GIRLHOOD

CHRISTINE E RAY

BUT YOU DON'T
LOOK SICK

The Real Life Adventures of Fibro Bitches, Lupus Warriors,
and other Superheroes Battling Invisible Illness

An Indie Blu(e) Publishing Anthology

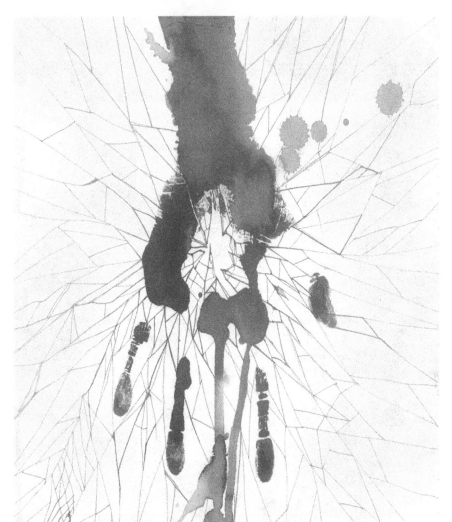

THROUGH THE LOOKING GLASS
REFLECTING ON MADNESS AND CHAOS WITHIN

An Indie Blu(e) Publishing Anthology

As the World Burns
Writers and Artists Reflect on a World Gone Mad

An Indie Blu(e) Publishing Anthology

Indie

Blu(e)

Indie Blu(e) Publishing is a progressive, feminist micro-press, committed to producing honest and thought-provoking works. Our anthologies are meant to celebrate diversity and raise awareness. The editors all passionately advocate for human rights; mental health awareness; chronic illness awareness; sexual abuse survivors; and LGBTQ+ equality. It is our mission, and a great honor, to provide platforms for those voices that are stifled and stigmatized.

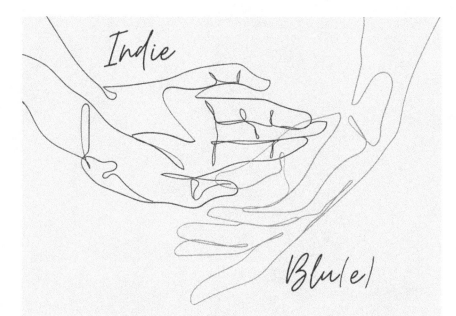

Indie Blu(e)

Indie Blu(e) Publishing wants your best and most incisive work. We are welcoming to all artists/writers regardless of race, orientation, gender, gender expression/identity, body type, ability, religious beliefs, income, or immigration status. We are actively seeking submissions from under-represented voices, including artists/authors who are Black, Brown, women, indigenous, gender-nonconforming, people with disabilities, lgbtqia+, and neurodivergent.

We will not accept/publish pieces that depict gratuitous violence, racism, sexism, homophobia, transphobia, xenophobia, and/or hate speech.

Printed in the USA
CPSIA information can be obtained
at www.ICGtesting.com
LVHW091150031023
759923LV00008B/20